Clever Quilts Encore

SUSAN TEEGARDEN DISSMORE

Martingale®
& COMPANY

CREDITS

President: Nancy J. Martin
CEO: Daniel J. Martin
Publisher: Jane Hamada
Editorial Director: Mary V. Green
Managing Editor: Tina Cook
Technical Editor: Ellen Pahl
Copy Editor: Liz McGehee
Design Director: Stan Green
Illustrator: Robin Strobel
Assistant Illustrator: Lisa McKenney
Cover and Text Designer: Trina Stahl
Photographer: Brent Kane

MISSION STATEMENT

Dedicated to providing quality products and service to inspire creativity.

Clever Quilts Encore
© 2003 Susan Teegarden Dissmore

Martingale®
& COMPANY

That Patchwork Place®

That Patchwork Place® is an imprint of
Martingale & Company®.

Martingale & Company
20205 144th Avenue NE
Woodinville, WA 98072-8478
www.martingale-pub.com

Printed in China
08 07 06 05 04   8 7 6 5 4 3 2

Library of Congress Cataloging-in-Publication Data

Dissmore, Susan Teegarden
    Clever quilts encore / Susan Teegarden Dissmore.
        p. cm.
    ISBN 1-56477-510-0
    1. Patchwork–Patterns. 2. Textile fabrics. 3. Patchwork quilts.
I. Title.
    TT835 . D576 2003
    746 .46'041–dc21
                                                2003008959

Dedication

To my husband, Tim, and to my sons, Blake and Justin

Acknowledgments

Writing a book is a collaborative effort. Although I am the one who sits in front of the computer entering the text, there are many people behind the scenes who have helped make this project come alive. Without their contributions, wonderful fabrics would not be available, patterns would not be adequately tested, and deadlines would not be met.

I would first like to acknowledge Lorri Gellerson, who has been here with me since the beginning of time! She helped me choose fabric and honestly critiqued my work. I don't know where I'd be without her.

Then there are my favorite machine quilters, Eileen Peacher and Sue Gantt. They were willing to drop what they were doing to help me complete the final quilts for this book. I would also like to thank Ginger Lundberg, a loyal customer and friend, who graciously volunteered to sew and bind two of the quilts in this book.

I would be sunk without my favorite fabric manufacturers. South Sea Imports, Moda Fabrics, and RJR Fashion Fabrics continue to produce the most whimsical and suitable theme fabrics for my "clever" quilting projects.

Thanks to all of my loyal customers who have purchased my books, patterns, and kits. Your continued support cannot go unmentioned. Last, but not least, I must acknowledge Martingale & Company for taking a chance with my book projects. None of this would have happened without their support of my work!

CONTENTS

INTRODUCTION

WONDERFUL PANEL, BORDER, and theme print fabrics seem to be spilling into quilt shops, creating endless possibilities for new and exciting quilts. There are so many great fabrics available that it becomes hard to choose. As a quilt designer and shop owner, I am constantly bombarded by the overabundance of great fabric choices, and I have spent many sleepless nights, my head spinning with new design ideas that use these fabrics.

New in this book is the use of a "cheater" crib panel. These panels are terrific when you need a quick-and-easy baby shower gift, but have you ever thought of cutting one apart to create a larger, unique quilt? The designs in this book do just that! I have cut the cheater panel apart and incorporated the cut pieces into a larger quilt. By adding simple blocks, the panel goes from simple to sublime. No more cheating with this fabric!

To expand your repertoire of design choices, this book also offers new setting options for the standard pillow panel as well as theme prints, border prints, and smaller panel squares. Many of the new designs are easy enough for the beginner, with a few that are challenging enough for the seasoned quilter.

Necessary to a stunning quilt is the appropriate mix of fabrics. Fabrics can make or break your project. In this book, I explain why some fabrics work and others don't. I love scrappy quilts, so many of the projects use fat quarters. This may be a good opportunity to clean out that fabric cupboard. Maybe you have even stashed away some of the fabrics I describe! If you want to make a statement with your quilt, then the information about planning your quilt is essential reading.

I know that once you get started with these fun fabrics, it will be hard to stop! Enjoy your ongoing journey with clever quilting!

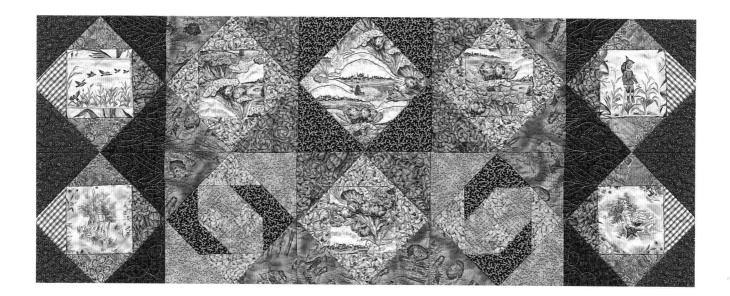

PANELS, BORDERS, AND THEME PRINTS REVISITED

I F LEFT FOLDED on a shelf with other fabrics, they can easily go unnoticed. But when you start looking, they seem to be everywhere. They can be realistic or touched with whimsy, framed in a box or flowing freely over the cloth, or they might even be placed in repeating rows. These wonderful fabrics are panels, borders, and theme prints.

Panel Prints

WHAT DOES your mind conjure up when you hear the words "panel print"? Before I became immersed in this subject, I would visualize a 36" x 42" piece of fabric that had a large whimsical animal placed in the center with cute pictures creating a framed border. I call these "cheater" panels.

Panel prints can, in fact, be exactly what I just described. But, there's more. Cheater panels can actually have various-sized images in "blocks" within that 36" x 42" area. Simply quilting and binding them could create a nice-looking, easy quilt, but the thought of cutting them apart was so intriguing that I just couldn't resist experimenting with them. See the quilts "Baby Crackers" on page 27, "Snow Crackers" on page 32, and "Firecrackers" on page 33 for the results of that experimentation.

In my first book, *Clever Quilts,* I defined panel prints as those with at least two square images in a selvage-to-selvage cut (often called pillow panels) and those with rectangular panel prints (suitable for a cloth book). This book includes those types of panels in the quilts "Forever Friends" on page 59 and "Once upon a Time" on page 72. There is another type of print that I also call a panel. These prints have

This Fourth of July "cheater" panel features a large central picture surrounded by smaller images of varying sizes and bordered at the top and bottom with long, rectangular images.

This panel fabric features birds in rectangles measuring 5" x 5½" and placed in rows from selvage to selvage.

blocked images placed in rows in a selvage-to-selvage cut. The images are typically 5" to 6" square, but can also be rectangular in shape. These smaller panels were used in the quilts "Birds of a Feather" on page 45.

Theme Prints

THEME PRINTS feature overall designs of a particular subject. They can be arranged in a directional pattern or just tossed about the cloth. They come in all sorts of shapes and sizes. Of the three types of fabrics, theme prints are the most versatile to use and can be adapted into most any type of quilt. They can be used as stand-alone blocks or incorporated as components of pieced blocks.

The scale of theme prints can vary greatly. I consider an image of 3" or less to be a small-scale print and an image of 6" or more a large-scale print. Anything in between is a medium-scale print. A variety of medium-scale theme prints (including tone-on-tone theme prints) were featured in the quilt "All Roads

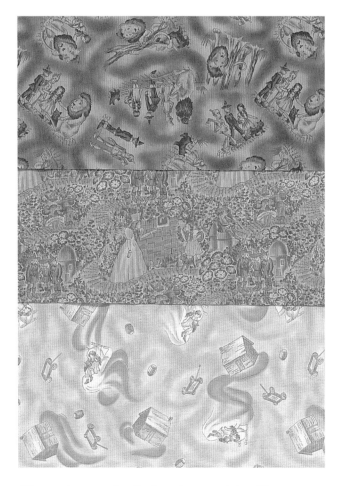

Theme prints come in all colors, shapes, and sizes. They can sometimes be tone-on-tone fabrics.

Images on this fabric could be considered large-scale, as they are easily placed in a square 6" or larger.

Lead to Oz" on page 22. Several medium-scale theme prints were used in the quilt "Child's Play" on page 49. "Frogs for the Boys" on page 53 features a frog theme fabric that I consider to be large-scale, even though the square was cut down to a size smaller than 6".

Border Prints

BORDER PRINTS are fabrics with images printed in "stripes" or borders along the lengthwise grain of the fabric. Each unique row is typically repeated two to three times across the width of the fabric. Whether whimsical or juvenile, I rarely use these prints as complete borders for a quilt, but I love to use them as pieces within the quilt. Such border prints were used in the quilts "Forever Friends" on page 59 and "Give Me Liberty" on page 68.

Another type of border print is one that also runs on the lengthwise grain of the fabric, but is repeated over and over again. These types of border prints are typically more elegant in nature. Such a border print was used in the quilt "Versailles" on page 77.

This patriotic border print fills the entire width of the fabric with the prints repeated twice.

PLANNING YOUR OWN CLEVER QUILT

THIS SECTION EXPLAINS my basic design approach and what you need to think about when adapting your fabrics to fit into the designs presented in this book. Yardage amounts listed with each of the projects will help you determine how much fabric to purchase.

Measuring the Designs

WHEN DESIGNING a quilt around a panel or theme print fabric, I first measure the print to determine an appropriate block size. The panel or theme print can become a block itself or it can be incorporated into a pieced block. To use your print in a quilt, look for quilts and blocks that have a large "blank" spot. Measure the designs in your chosen fabric, and compare those measurements to the blank spots. For each of the quilts in this book, look at the finished block and panel sizes listed within each set of directions to determine if your fabric will fit easily.

Adapting Fabrics

YOU'VE CHOSEN your design from the book and found a fabric that you want to use, but the preliminary measurements of the images indicate that the fabric is smaller than the blank spot you want to fill. Consider adding coping strips, filler strips, or coping triangles to bring the images up to the size required.

Coping Strips

Coping strips work like frames. Use them to completely surround fabric cut from a panel, border, or theme print when it needs to be enlarged. For example,

if you have a panel that has an unfinished measurement of 10½" square and it needs to be 12½" square, you can add 1½"-wide coping strips to all sides of the square, using a ¼" seam allowance, to achieve the desired size.

10½" cut
10" finished

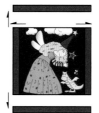
12½" unfinished
12" finished

Add 1½"-wide coping strips to all sides.

Filler Strips

I define a filler strip as a piece of fabric used wherever there is a blank space to fill. The blank space may only be on one side of a panel, border, or theme print; or it can be on as many as three sides. The filler strips can be pieced or unpieced. I used both pieced filler strips and unpieced filler strips in "Firecrackers" on page 33.

Three Unpieced Filler Strips

One Pieced Filler Strip

Coping Triangles

Coping triangles are half-square triangles added to the sides of a panel or theme print square to create a larger square. Coping triangles can be especially helpful when you replace a panel print with a theme print.

When filling a square space of a specific size with a center square plus coping triangles, you will need to do some math. To calculate the size of the center square, divide the desired finished size of the block by 1.414, rounding to the nearest ⅛" (use the chart that follows to convert your decimal to a fraction). Then add ½" for seam allowances. For example, if you want a finished-size block of 8" square, divide 8 by 1.414. This equals 5.657, which you will round to 5⅝". Add ½" seam allowances and cut the center square to 6⅛" x 6⅛".

Decimal to Fraction Equivalents

.125 = ⅛"
.25 = ¼"
.375 = ⅜"
.5 = ½"
.625 = ⅝"
.75 = ¾"
.875 = ⅞"

To calculate the measurement of the squares to be cut in half for the coping triangles, first divide the desired finished size of the block in half, then add ⅞". Using the example of a finished-size 8" square, divide 8 in half, yielding 4". Add ⅞", and cut a 4⅞" square. For each center square, cut two squares to this measurement. Then cut each square in half diagonally once to yield four coping triangles.

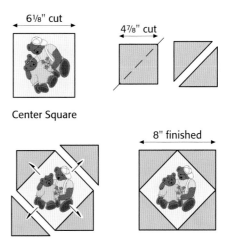

Center Square

The following chart includes common finished-block sizes and dimensions for their accompanying center squares and coping triangles.

Finished Block Size	Size to Cut Center Square	Size to Cut Square for Coping Triangles
4"	3⅜" x 3⅜"	2⅞" x 2⅞"
6"	4¾" x 4¾"	3⅞" x 3⅞"
8"	6⅛" x 6⅛"	4⅞" x 4⅞"
12"	9" x 9"	6⅞" x 6⅞"

Choosing and Preparing Fabrics

EVEN THE simplest block or quilt design can become a stunning quilt by choosing just the right fabrics. Although it may seem like a daunting task, it truly can be fun and rewarding. The best thing to do is just enjoy the process. To start, choose the panel, border, or theme print fabric (see pages 7–9). Once you have chosen the main fabric, the job of selecting coordinates becomes a little easier. Use 100%-cotton fabric; it is easy to handle and presses well.

The light and dark prints coordinate well with the theme print and are repeated in different colorways in this grouping.

Choosing Coordinating Fabric

Always look for cotton fabrics that will enhance the artwork of the panel, border, or theme print. Remember that if the original coordinating fabrics from the collection are no longer available, you can use any fabric from any collection as long as it complements the main print.

When making preliminary coordinating fabric choices, look for both the dominant and subtle colors within the theme design itself. If you find a color you don't like in the print, either ignore it altogether or just add a small amount of it in your quilt. Also try to vary the print, scale, and value of the fabrics in your preliminary choices.

With that being said, don't worry about following any hard-and-fast rules. If you find fabrics that work well with the theme print, just go with your instincts. When I was choosing fabrics for the quilt "Best Friends" on page 39, I used several fabrics with the same print but in different colorways. I repeated the same print in both the light and dark fabrics used in the Four Patch blocks. I liked it, so I went with those choices. It worked, and worked well. Remember that this is your creation. Trust yourself. If you like it, do it!

Scrappy quilts are my favorites, so I tend to work with lots of fabrics when creating quilts. With the main print in hand, I build a large stack of coordinating fabrics that I think might work in the design. Once the stack is built, I narrow down the possibilities to my favorite pieces. This process occurs as I decide where to place the fabric within each of the blocks. Unused fabrics are filed in my fabric closet for future use. If you are uncomfortable choosing coordinates, view this as an excellent opportunity to experiment with new fabric combinations. The more you practice, the better you will become!

When building my preliminary stack of fabric, I typically start with half-yard cuts because they are easily converted to fat quarters—my favorite cut! Although fat quarters are my first choice, they will not work for everything. The yardage requirements for the quilts in this book will specify when a fat quarter is appropriate.

When choosing fabric, there is one rule of thumb that I rarely break: Always accent a light background piece with a darker piece. If your theme fabric has a light background, it is best to make the fabric next to it dark. If your theme fabric has a darker background, the fabric next to it should be either very dark or light. By following this rule, you will help accentuate the theme print.

Preparing Fabric

I recommend prewashing all fabrics prior to their use in any quilt project. I have found that fabrics will shrink at different rates and sometimes lose color. By prewashing, you may prevent a disaster later on. Wash your fabrics on the gentle cycle with like colors and remove them from the dryer while they are still a bit damp. If desired, add spray sizing or starch when you press to restore some of the body and crispness that was lost during the washing process. The sizing or starch will make it easier to control your fabrics while cutting, sewing, and pressing seams.

Once your fabric is prewashed, you may have only 40" to 42" of usable fabric from selvage to selvage (or 20" to 21" if using fat quarters). In the project instructions, all cross-grain cuts have been listed as 21" or 42" in width; the yardage requirements have been calculated based on 40" of usable fabric width, so you should have adequate fabric.

QUILTMAKING BASICS

YOUR FABRIC IS chosen and prewashed, but before you begin, gather your tools and supplies and review the following quiltmaking basics.

Tools and Supplies

Sewing Machine

First and foremost, you need a sewing machine that is in good working order. Keep your machine lint-free and well oiled (if necessary). Your machine need not be fancy, just your friend. Get to know how it operates. The more you know about your machine, the better.

The stitch quality on your machine is also important. You want your stitch to be even on both sides of the fabric—not too tight or too loose. A tight tension may cause puckering; a loose tension will cause your stitch to come apart. Have your machine serviced by a professional periodically to keep it in good working order. Once that is done, set up your machine for straight stitching. A setting of 12 to 14 stitches per inch is adequate for machine piecing your quilt top.

Rotary Cutter and Mat

A medium- to large-size rotary cutter is an essential tool for the projects in this book. In addition to the rotary cutter, you will need a self-healing mat. Your mat should measure at least 18" x 24".

Rulers

For rotary cutting, you'll need rulers. The sizes I find most helpful are 6" x 24" for cutting strips from 42"-wide fabric, 6" x 12" for cutting strips from fat quarters, and assorted square rulers for cutting squares

and squaring up blocks. Square rulers come in various sizes. I prefer and use the 6½", 8", 9½", and 12½" square rulers. If you need to purchase these and don't want to invest in all of them right away, start with the larger ones.

Template Plastic

I use template plastic to aid in selective cutting. I have squares in various sizes that I keep just for this process. Specific use is discussed in "Selective Cutting" on page 15.

Other Basic Sewing Supplies

You will also need basic sewing supplies, including scissors for cutting thread, a seam ripper, straight pins, a good-quality cotton thread, and basic sewing-machine needles. I use size 80/12 universal or size 70/10 jeans/denim needles for machine piecing.

Rotary Cutting

BEFORE YOU begin to cut strips from your fabrics, you will need to straighten the edges.

1. Fold your fabric in half from selvage to selvage. Holding the selvage edges together, hold your fabric out in front of you, letting the fabric hang freely. Move the selvage edges until the fabric hangs wrinkle-free. Carefully lay the folded fabric on your rotary mat.

2. Line up a square ruler along the folded edge, and place a 6" x 24" (or 6" x 12" for fat quarters) ruler to the left of the square. Remove the square ruler and cut away a small portion of the left side

of the fabric. If you are left-handed, reverse this process. You now have a clean, straight edge from which to cut strips.

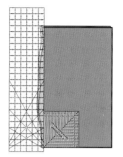

3. To cut strips, move the 6" x 24" ruler to the right, matching the ruler line for the desired width to the freshly cut edges. Cut a strip. Repeat until you have the desired number of strips.

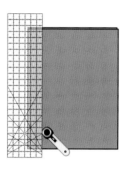

Selective Cutting

When working with panels, borders, and theme prints, you will often need to center a desired motif within a shape, such as a square or rectangle. I recommend using translucent template plastic when centering a motif.

1. Cut a piece of template plastic to the finished size of the square or rectangle desired. Draw an **X** on the template plastic, with lines connecting opposite corners and crossing at the center. You can draw additional lines to indicate other piecing (such as diagonal lines at the corners for coping triangles).

2. Place the template plastic on your fabric and move it around until you have centered the desired motif to your satisfaction. Using a ruler and rotary

cutter, add ¼" on each side of the template plastic and cut. I place my ruler carefully over the template plastic when cutting.

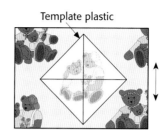

Selective Cutting of Theme Print

Machine Piecing

Grab a comfortable chair and get an iron and ironing board ready. It's time to start sewing your quilt!

Maintaining the ¼" Seam

All of the cutting directions in this book include a ¼"-wide seam allowance. To achieve the best results in machine piecing, maintain a straight, scant ¼" seam throughout the project. Every aspect of your quilt top will be affected if you do not maintain that seam allowance.

What is a straight, scant ¼" seam? A scant seam is one that is at least one to two threads smaller than an actual ¼". This allows for the space that is taken up by the thread and fabric when you press the seam to one side. To keep your seams straight, I highly recommend the use of a ¼" machine presser foot. If you do not have a foot available, use an adhesive product, such as ¼" masking tape or moleskin that can be attached to the bed of your machine (not on the feed dogs). Once you have attached the foot or adhesive guide, check for accuracy by holding a ruler next to the raw edge of your fabric. The thread should be just inside the ¼" line of your ruler. Adjust the position of your needle or adhesive guide until you have achieved the desired seam width.

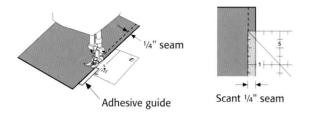

¼" seam

Adhesive guide

Scant ¼" seam

Pressing

Pressing after sewing each seam helps ensure the accuracy of your piecing. Most often, you will press seams to one side and usually toward the darker fabric. Occasionally, you may need to press a seam open to eliminate bulk. Press with a hot, dry iron set for cotton. Although I like a little steam, it can cause stretching. Be careful if you choose to apply steam to your pieces. As you press, try to plan ahead so you will have opposing seams within your quilt blocks and rows of your quilt top. By doing this, your seams will butt up against each other, allowing you to match seam intersections perfectly.

Opposing Seams

Chain Piecing

Chain piecing is a process of feeding layered pairs of patches or strips through your sewing machine one after another. It is fast and efficient, eliminating the need to continually snip threads and thread tails. Once you have finished a chain-pieced set, feed a small piece of scrap fabric through the machine as the last piece. Snip your thread and transfer the chain of joined pieces to your pressing surface.

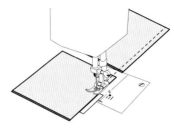

Sewing Strip Sets

Throughout this book, you will be instructed to sew strip sets. A strip set consists of two or more strips that are sewn together along their long edges. They can then be crosscut and used alone or sewn to other crosscut units to form blocks or components of blocks. Blocks that can be made from strip sets include the Four Patch, Rail Fence, and Nine Patch. On occasion, you may be instructed to "unsew" or remove parts of strip sets with a seam ripper to obtain the required number of units.

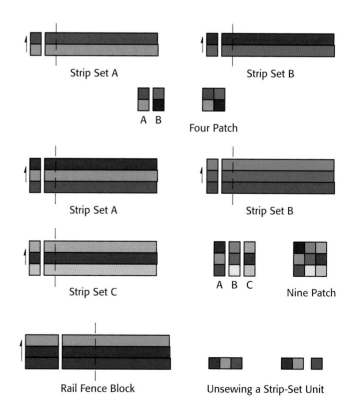

Strip Set A

Strip Set B

A B

Four Patch

Strip Set A

Strip Set B

Strip Set C

A B C

Nine Patch

Rail Fence Block

Unsewing a Strip-Set Unit

Working with Triangles

Several of the blocks featured in this book will include triangles. Since most of my quilts are scrappy, I tend to cut triangles from squares and sew them back together individually. Extra care must be taken when sewing triangles because the center cut will be on the bias. Since bias tends to stretch, let your machine's feed dogs do all the work when sewing triangles. Triangles can be sewn into pieced rows as shown, sewn into half-square-triangle units, or used as a patch within a block.

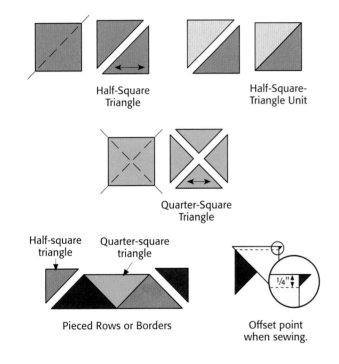

Half-Square Triangle

Half-Square-Triangle Unit

Quarter-Square Triangle

Half-square triangle   Quarter-square triangle

Pieced Rows or Borders

1/4"

Offset point when sewing.

Squaring Up Blocks

When stitching components of blocks, I press and trim as I go. If a block is made up of half-square triangles, for instance, I will press the seam and trim the half-square triangle to the desired unfinished size, even if it's just a few threads. That way, when it is sewn into the finished block, it is nearly perfect. I say "nearly perfect" because absolute perfection is unachievable and not necessary in my mind.

After stitching all the patches of your quilt blocks together, press and trim again if needed. Use a large square ruler to measure them and make sure they are the desired size plus a ¼" seam allowance on each edge. For example, if you are making 12" blocks, they should measure 12½" before you sew them together. Be consistent with this step, making sure that all your blocks are the same measurement. If your blocks are not the required size, you will need to adjust all other components of the quilt accordingly.

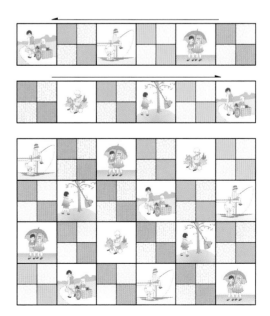

Setting Blocks Together

Blocks are typically arranged in rows before being sewn together. Pin the blocks together at intersections to ensure that your seams line up properly. Stitch the blocks together row by row and press all the seams in one direction. Press seams in opposite directions from row to row for easier matching. Stitch the rows together.

Adding Borders

FOR BEST results, do not cut border strips and sew them to the quilt without measuring the quilt top first. The edges of the quilt may have stretched during construction. I take three measurements and average them when determining the length of the border strips. The three measurements consist of the center and each side, both top to bottom and side to side.

In addition to accurate measurements, I find that cutting the border strips on the straight of grain, or parallel to the selvage edge, is most helpful in keeping the borders from stretching. I don't always cut inner borders on the straight of grain, but I do this on the outer borders whenever possible.

DIRECTIONAL PRINT BORDERS

To cut border strips from a directional print, first measure and cut the top and bottom borders on the cross grain, or selvage to selvage. Cut as many strips as needed and piece if necessary. Sew these to the quilt top first. Then measure and cut the side borders on the straight grain, parallel to the selvage edge. Sew the side borders to the quilt top last for greatest stability.

For nondirectional fabrics, I sew the side borders to the quilt first; then I add the top and bottom borders. Be sure to pin the borders before sewing. I start pinning at the ends and work toward the center of the quilt. If the quilt is slightly larger than the border strip, ease the quilt to match the length of the border strip when stitching. To do this, place the quilt top on the bed of your machine, with the wrong side of the border strip facing you. This allows the feed dogs to do their job; they will move the lower layer along at a slightly faster speed than the top layer. Always handle border strips carefully to avoid stretching.

Finishing Your Quilt

AT THIS point, you need to decide how you will quilt your project and if you will need to mark the quilting designs on your quilt top. Although marking is not necessary for stitching in the ditch and some free-motion quilting, a complex design may need to be marked on the quilt top before the top is layered with batting and backing.

With 42"-wide fabric, most quilts in this book will require a pieced backing. Prewash and remove all selvage edges from your backing fabric before you sew the pieces together. The backing and batting should be 2" to 4" larger all around each edge of the finished quilt top.

Assembling the Quilt Sandwich

The next step is to make the quilt "sandwich," which consists of the backing, batting, and quilt top. Your batting choice will hinge on whether you choose to machine or hand quilt. Check with your local quilt shop to determine the perfect batting for your project.

1. Lay the backing fabric, wrong side up, on a smooth, clean surface. Keep the backing fabric smooth and wrinkle-free but not stretched. Secure the backing to the surface with masking tape or binder clips.

2. Lay the batting over the backing. Starting from the center, smooth out the batting until there are no wrinkles.

3. Lay the quilt top, right side up, over the batting. Starting from the center, smooth out the quilt top over the batting.

4. Pin or hand-baste the layers together. Since I machine quilt, I use #1 safety pins for large quilts and a basting spray for small quilts. Begin pinning in the center of the quilt and work toward the outer edges. Placement of pins will depend on the type of machine quilting you plan to do, but place them no more than 3" apart. If you plan to hand quilt, thread basting is a better choice. Sew a large grid of stitches using a cotton thread. Begin in the center of the quilt and stitch about 4" to 6" apart in all directions. Make the final stitches around the outer edges of the quilt.

5. Machine or hand quilt as desired.

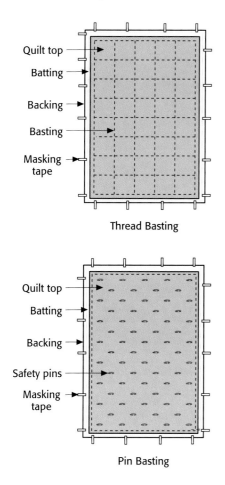

Quilt top
Batting
Backing
Basting
Masking tape

Thread Basting

Quilt top
Batting
Backing
Safety pins
Masking tape

Pin Basting

Binding and Finishing

Binding is the final step in completing your quilt. I cut binding strips on the cross grain, 2½" x 42", to make a ½"-wide finished binding. For a narrower binding, cut narrower strips. If you plan to hang your quilt, make a hanging sleeve before binding. That way, you can sew it onto the quilt as you stitch the binding.

Adding a Hanging Sleeve

1. Cut a 5"- to 9"-wide strip (or piece multiple strips) of fabric equal to the width of your quilt top minus 2". Press each end under ¼". Press under ¼" again and stitch ⅛" from the folded edges.

2. Fold the strip in half lengthwise with wrong sides together. Pin it together at the ends and at several points in between. Press.

CLEVER TIP

Press a small pleat in the hanging sleeve before hand stitching it to the backing. That will add some extra fullness to accommodate the rod so that the rod won't make a bulge on the front of your quilt when you hang it.

3. Center the sleeve on the back of the quilt, aligning the raw edges with the raw edges of the quilt top. Pin in place and stitch by machine ⅛" from the raw edge. The top of the sleeve will be stitched again when the binding is applied, and the raw edges will be covered when the binding is folded over and stitched down.

4. After binding, hand stitch the bottom edge of the sleeve to the quilt back. Be careful to catch only the backing and batting and leave the ends of the sleeve open.

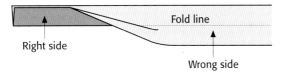

Binding

1. Cut enough strips to go around the edges of your quilt, with an extra 12" for turning corners and joining the ends. Sew the strips together with diagonal seams, forming one continuous strip. Press the seams open.

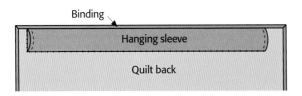

2. Press the binding strip in half lengthwise, wrong sides together.

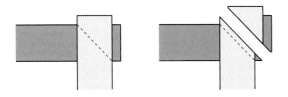

3. Position the binding all the way around the quilt, making sure that none of the seams fall at the corners of the quilt.

4. Leaving an 8" to 10" tail at the beginning, sew the binding to the quilt top with a ¼" seam allowance.

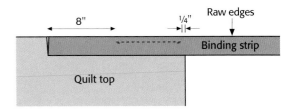

5. When you approach a corner, stop ¼" away from it. Backstitch and remove the quilt from the machine. Turn the quilt so that you will be stitching down the next side. Fold the binding up, parallel to the side of the quilt, at a 45° angle. Then fold the strip down so that the fold is parallel to the top edge of the quilt and the raw edges are aligned with the side edge of the quilt. Begin sewing from the top with a ¼" seam allowance.

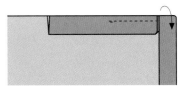

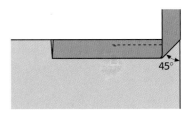

6. Continue in this manner around the quilt, stopping 8" to 10" from where you began stitching. Backstitch and remove the quilt from the machine. Trim the binding so that the beginning and ending tails overlap by 2½". (The overlap should equal the width that you cut your binding strips.)

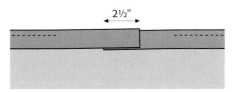

7. Open and place the strips, right sides together, at right angles. Stitch on the diagonal and trim away the excess fabric. Press the seam open. Refold the binding and finish sewing it to the quilt.

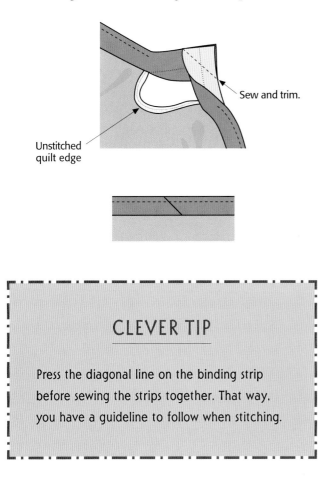

Sew and trim.

Unstitched quilt edge

CLEVER TIP

Press the diagonal line on the binding strip before sewing the strips together. That way, you have a guideline to follow when stitching.

8. Bring the binding from the front of the quilt to the back and, if desired, pin it in place. Using a thread that matches the binding, whipstitch the folded edge to the back of the quilt. Be careful that your stitches do not go through to the front of the quilt. As you approach a corner, pull the binding out. With your thumbnail in the corner, fold over the unstitched binding edge, creating a miter. Secure it with stitches. Repeat for the remaining corners.

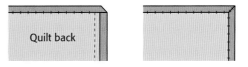

Quilt back

Adding a Label

This step takes only a few minutes and is well worth the effort. Adding a label will document information about your quilt. The label can be elaborate or plain. I like to use preprinted labels, as they are both decorative and easy to use. Using a permanent ink pen, I simply write the name of the quilt, my name, the quilter's name (if applicable), the date it was completed, and the place where it was completed. I fold under the edges of the label and whipstitch it into place. It's that simple.

All Roads Lead to Oz

Designed, sewn, and quilted by Susan Dissmore, 2002.

About This Quilt

Finished quilt: 40" x 40"

Finished block: 8" x 8"

Finished theme print square: 4" x 4"

In addition to sewing and designing quilts, I have another passion: collecting dolls. This quilt was created to complement my collection of Wizard of Oz dolls. The gold in the Snail's Trail block creates the yellow brick road that leads you to the center of the quilt—Emerald City in the Land of Oz. Change the theme print and the colors to create your own story quilt!

Materials

Yardages are based on 42"-wide fabric.

- 1 fat quarter of theme print 1 for blocks A and B
- 1 fat quarter of theme print 2 for block D
- 1 fat quarter of theme print 3 for block D
- ½ yard of dark blue for blocks D and E
- 1 fat quarter of blue tone-on-tone theme print for block E
- 1 fat quarter of medium gold for blocks C and E
- 1 fat quarter of dark gold for blocks C and E
- 1 fat quarter of medium green tone-on-tone print for blocks B and C
- 1 fat quarter of medium green print for blocks A and C
- 1 fat quarter of dark green for block D
- 1 fat quarter of medium blue for blocks D and E
- 1 fat quarter of blue gingham check for blocks D and E
- 1 fat quarter of pink floral for block B
- 1 fat quarter of dark pink for blocks B and D
- 2⅞ yards of fabric for backing
- ½ yard of fabric for binding
- 48" x 48" piece of batting

Block A   Block B   Block C

Block D   Block E

Cutting

All measurements include ¼" seam allowance.

From theme print 1, selectively cut:
- 1 square, 6⅛" x 6⅛", on point*
- 4 squares, 4½" x 4½"

From theme prints 2 and 3, selectively cut a total of:
- 12 squares, 4½" x 4½"

From the blue tone-on-tone theme print, selectively cut:
- 4 squares, 4½" x 4½"

From the medium gold, cut:
- 1 strip, 2" x 21"
- 1 strip, 3⅝" x 21". From it, cut 4 squares, 3⅝" x 3⅝"; cut the squares in half diagonally once to yield 8 triangles.

See page 15 for information about selective cutting on point.

8. Using the blue tone-on-tone theme print squares, the medium blue and blue gingham check triangles, and the 4⅞" medium gold, dark gold, and dark blue triangles, make block E in the same manner as described for blocks A and B. Rotate the placement of the triangles as shown.

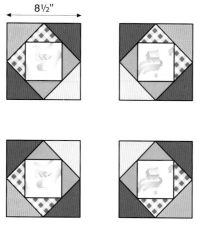

8½"

Block E
Make 1 of each.

9. Arrange the blocks as shown in the diagram at right. Sew the blocks together in rows. Press the rows in opposite directions.

10. Sew the rows together to form the quilt top.

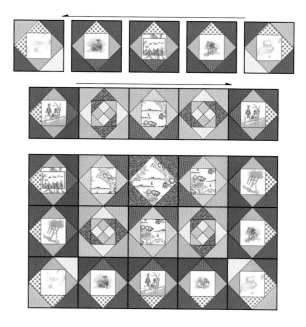

11. Quilt as desired and bind. Refer to "Finishing Your Quilt" on page 18 for more details if needed. This quilt was machine quilted using free-motion techniques. The center theme prints were outline quilted, and the blocks were accented with leaf and mosaic patterns.

OTHER OPTIONS

Any smaller panel print with a finished measurement of 4" x 4" could be substituted for the theme print squares. To adjust the center of block A, simply add coping triangles to the panel square. By changing the theme prints and the colors, you can create your own quilt tale!

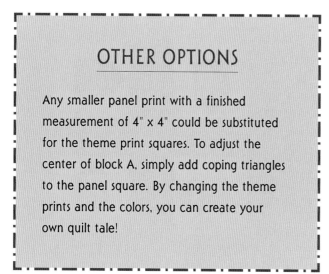

Baby Crackers

Designed, sewn, and quilted by Susan Dissmore, 2002.

About This Quilt

Finished quilt: 48" x 60"
Finished Rail Fence block: 4" x 4"
Finished small Star block: 4" x 4"
Finished large Star block: 8" x 8"

No "cheating" needed with this design! Start with any cheater panel that has varied-sized images and a dark center. Then cut it apart and add coping strips to the cheater blocks as needed. Easy Rail Fence and Star blocks complete the design to make a cuddly crib quilt. It's the best of both worlds: easy piecing and a fun, irresistible panel print. (See "Firecrackers" on page 33 if you have a panel fabric with a light center design.)

Materials

Yardages are based on 42"-wide fabric.

♦ 1 panel with at least 9 varied-sized images (more is desirable)
♦ ½ yard of theme print for large rectangle blocks at top and bottom*
♦ 8 assorted fat quarters for Rail Fence blocks and filler squares
♦ 4 fat quarters of light beige for Star blocks and filler squares
♦ 4 assorted fat quarters for coping and filler strips
♦ 1 fat quarter of dark print for star points
♦ 3¼ yards of fabric for backing
♦ ⅝ yard of fabric for binding
♦ 56" x 68" piece of batting

You will need this fabric only if your panel print does not have horizontal images that will work in the 8" x 20" spaces of the quilt diagram.

Cutting

All measurements include ¼" seam allowance.

From the panel print or theme print, rough-cut:

♦ 1 center panel, approximately 9" x 13"
♦ 2 horizontal pieces, approximately 9" x 21"
♦ 2 squares, approximately 9" x 9"
♦ 6 rectangles, approximately 7" x 9"

From *each* of the 8 assorted fat quarters, cut:

♦ 9 strips, 1½" x 21"
♦ 1 strip, 2½" x 21"

From *each* of the 4 light beige fat quarters, cut:

♦ 3 strips, 2½" x 21"

From 1 light beige fat quarter, cut:

♦ 4 strips, 1½" x 21". From them, cut 16 rectangles, 1½" x 2½", and 16 squares, 1½" x 1½".

From 1 light beige fat quarter, cut:

♦ 3 strips, 2½" x 21". From them, cut 8 rectangles, 2½" x 4½", and 8 squares, 2½" x 2½".

From *each* of the 4 assorted fat quarters, cut:

♦ 2 strips, 2½" x 21"
♦ Coping strips as needed

From 1 of the assorted fat quarters, cut:

♦ 4 squares, 2½" x 2½" (for the small Star block center)*

From the dark print fat quarter, cut:

♦ 3 strips, 1½" x 21". From them, cut 32 squares, 1½" x 1½".

♦ 2 strips, 2½" x 21". From them, cut 16 squares, 2½" x 2½".

You may want to fussy cut designs from your fabric to feature in the center of the Star blocks as I did.

Assembly

1. Using the 1½" x 21" strips cut from the eight assorted fat quarters, arrange them into two groups of four strips each to make nine strip sets of each fabric combination. Group them in an order that is pleasing to you. Sew the strips together into strip sets. Press. Crosscut the strip sets into a total of 68 segments, 4½" wide, to make the Rail Fence blocks.

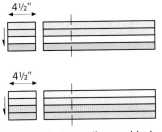

Cut a total of 68 Rail Fence blocks.

2. Sew the 2½" x 21" light beige strips together to form three strip sets of four strips each. Crosscut the strip sets into 24 segments, 2½" wide. Sew 22 of the crosscut segments together, end to end, as shown. The remaining segments will be used as is.

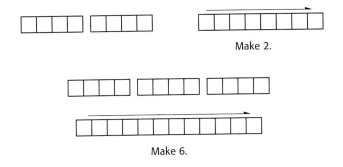

Make 2.

Make 6.

3. Trim the rough-cut center panel to 8½" x 12½". Add coping strips if needed (refer to page 10). Arrange the strip-set segments, Rail Fence blocks, and center panel as shown. Sew the center section together.

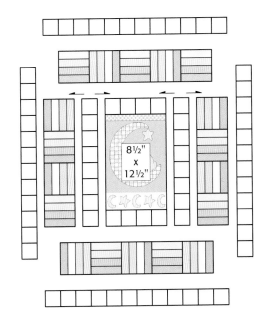

4. Trim the two widest panel pictures to 20½" x 8½". Add coping strips if needed.

5. Sew the 2½" x 21" strips cut from all 12 of the assorted fat quarters into four sets of four strips each. Crosscut the strip sets into 32 segments, 2½" wide. Sew the crosscut segments into two units of three segments each. Reserve the balance for later use.

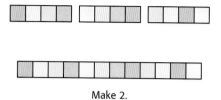

Make 2.

6. Sew the pieced units from steps 2 and 5 to all sides of the 20½" x 8½" pieces from step 4. Press. Add the Rail Fence blocks, alternating them as shown. Press.

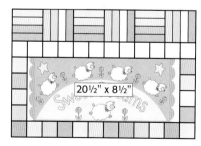

20½" x 8½"

20½" x 8½"

Make 1 of each.

7. With right sides together, place a dark 1½" square on one corner of a light beige 1½" x 2½" rectangle. Draw a diagonal line through the center of the square as shown and stitch on the drawn line. Trim away the excess fabric, leaving a ¼" seam allowance. Press. Repeat on the other side of the rectangle. Make 16 flying-geese units.

Make 16.

8. Using the flying-geese units from step 7, the 2½" center squares, and the light beige 1½" squares, sew the patches in rows for the small Star block. Press. Sew the rows together. Make four blocks that measure 4½" x 4½".

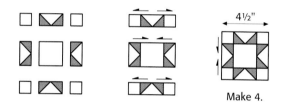

4½"

Make 4.

9. Unsew the center of six crosscut segments from step 5. Resew into six Four Patch blocks.

4½"

Make 6.

10. Sew a Four Patch block to one side of each of the small Star blocks as shown. Reserve the two remaining Four Patch blocks for the centers of the two large Star blocks.

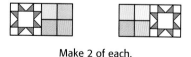

Make 2 of each.

11. Using the dark 2½" squares and the light beige 2½" x 4½" rectangles, refer to step 7 to make eight flying-geese units for the large Star blocks.

12. Using the two reserved Four Patch blocks for the center, the flying-geese units from step 11, and the 2½" light beige squares, sew the patches in rows for the large Star blocks. Press. Sew the rows together. Make two blocks that measure 8½" x 8½".

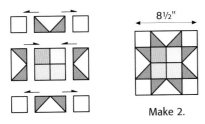

8½"

Make 2.

13. Add the Rail Fence blocks to the outside edges of the large Star blocks as shown. Press. Each unit should measure 12½" x 12½".

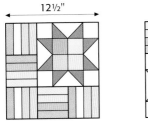

12½"

14. Trim two of the remaining panel images to 8½" x 8½". Add coping strips if needed. Add the Rail Fence blocks as shown. Press. Each unit should measure 12½" x 12½".

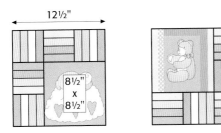

12½"

8½"
x
8½"

Make 1 of each.

15. Trim the remaining panel images to 6½" x 8½". Add coping strips if needed. Add the Rail Fence blocks, the Four Patch and small Star block units, and 10 crosscut segments from step 5 to form the units. Press. Each unit should measure 12½" x 12½".

12½"

6½"
x
8½"

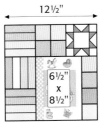

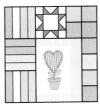

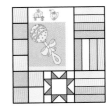

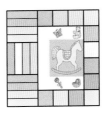

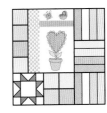

Make 1 of each.

ANOTHER OPTION

Snow Crackers

*48" x 61", designed, sewn, and quilted
by Susan Dissmore, 2002.*

I found a snowman panel fabric with a dark center that made it suitable for this wintry version of the "Baby Crackers" quilt design. The fabric had only one large 8" x 20" rectangle block available, so I substituted a theme print combined with the leftover strip-set pieces to create the large rectangle shape for the bottom of the quilt. I used fewer fabrics in this quilt—a total of four half-yard cuts instead of eight fat quarters for the Rail Fence blocks and filler squares.

16. Sew the quilt together in vertical rows. Sew the rows together to form the quilt top.

17. Quilt as desired and bind. Refer to "Finishing Your Quilt" on page 18 for more details if needed. This quilt was machine quilted; the border was quilted in a free-motion maze pattern, the small squares were crosshatched, and the remainder of the quilt was quilted in a free-form meandering pattern.

Firecrackers

Designed and sewn by Susan Dissmore, machine quilted by Sue Gantt, 2002.

About This Quilt

Finished quilt: 48" x 60"
Finished Rail Fence block: 4" x 4"
Finished small Star block: 4" x 4"
Finished large Star block: 8" x 8"

This quilt, a variation of "Baby Crackers" on page 27, was designed to feature a cheater panel with a light background. In addition to the larger block designs, this patriotic panel had several smaller block designs that were easily incorporated into the quilt. The traditional red-white-and-blue coloring in the panel was accented with Rail Fence blocks, using a variety of fat quarters of the same colors. The gold fabrics add the sparkle!

Materials

Yardages are based on 42"-wide fabric.

♦ 1 panel with at least 10 varied-sized images
♦ *Optional:* ½ yard of theme print for blocks
♦ 8 fat quarters of assorted blue prints for small Star blocks, Rail Fence blocks, and filler squares
♦ 8 fat quarters of assorted red prints for small Star blocks, Rail Fence blocks, and filler squares
♦ 4 fat quarters of light beige for Star blocks and filler squares
♦ 4 fat quarters of assorted gold prints for large Star blocks and filler squares
♦ 3¼ yards of fabric for backing
♦ ⅝ yard of fabric for binding
♦ 56" x 68" piece of batting

Cutting

All measurements include ¼" seam allowance.

From the panel print or theme print, rough-cut:

♦ 1 center panel, approximately 9" x 13"
♦ 2 horizontal pieces, approximately 21" x 9"
♦ 6 squares, approximately 5" x 5"
♦ 4 squares, approximately 9" x 9"
♦ 2 rectangles, approximately 7" x 9"

From *each* of the 8 blue fat quarters, cut:

♦ 4 strips, 1½" x 21"

From 4 of the blue fat quarters, cut:

♦ 1 strip, 2½" x 21"

From 1 blue fat quarter, cut:

♦ 2 strips, 1½" x 21". From them, cut 16 squares, 1½" x 1½".
♦ 2 squares, 2½" x 2½"

From *each* of the 8 red fat quarters, cut:

♦ 4 strips, 1½" x 21"

From 4 of the red fat quarters, cut:

♦ 1 strip, 2½" x 21"

From 1 red fat quarter, cut:

♦ 2 strips, 1½" x 21". From them, cut 16 squares, 1½" x 1½".
♦ 2 squares, 2½" x 2½"

From *each* of the 4 light beige fat quarters, cut:

♦ 2 strips, 2½" x 21"

From 1 light beige fat quarter, cut:

♦ 4 strips, 1½" x 21". From them, cut 16 rectangles, 1½" x 2½", and 16 squares, 1½" x 1½".

From 1 light beige fat quarter, cut:

♦ 3 strips, 2½" x 21". From them, cut 8 rectangles, 2½" x 4½", and 8 squares, 2½" x 2½".

From *each* of the 4 gold fat quarters, cut:

♦ 2 strips, 2½" x 21"
♦ 1 rectangle, 2½" x 6½"

From *each* of 2 gold fat quarters, cut:

♦ 1 rectangle, 2½" x 4½"
♦ 1 rectangle, 2½" x 8½"

From 1 gold fat quarter, cut:

♦ 2 strips, 2½" x 21". From them, cut 16 squares, 2½" x 2½".

Assembly

1. Using the 1½"-wide strips cut from the eight blue fat quarters, arrange and sew them together in groups of four to make eight strip sets. Crosscut the strip sets into 32 segments, 4½" wide, to make the Rail Fence blocks.

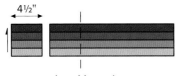

Make 8 blue strip sets.
Cut 32 Rail Fence blocks.

2. Repeat step 1, using the 1½"-wide strips cut from the eight red fat quarters.

3. Sew the 2½"-wide light beige strips together to make two strip sets of four strips each. Crosscut the strip sets into 12 segments, 2½" wide (reserve 2 segments). Sew the crosscut segments together, end to end, as shown.

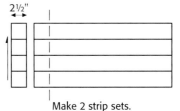

Make 2 strip sets.
Cut 12 segments.

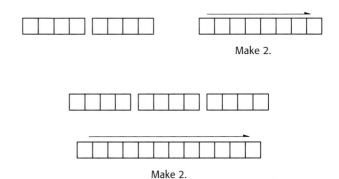

Make 2.

Make 2.

4. Sew the blue and red 2½"-wide strips into four strip sets of four strips each as shown. Crosscut the strip sets into 16 segments, 2½" wide (reserve 4 segments). Sew 12 of the crosscut segments together, end to end, as shown.

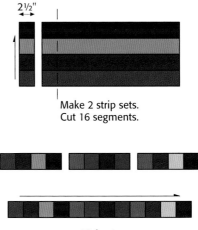

Make 2 strip sets.
Cut 16 segments.

Make 4.

5. Trim the light center panel to 8½" x 12½". Arrange the Rail Fence blocks and the pieced strip segments together as shown. Sew the center section together.

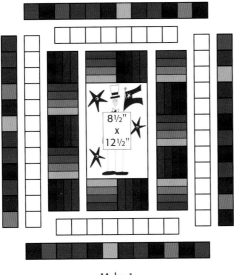

Make 1.

6. Trim the two widest panel pictures to 20½" x 8½". Add coping or filler strips if needed.

CLEVER TIP

To create your own "flag" for one of the rectangular spaces, piece or appliqué a small Star block. Add strips of red prints and white prints to fill the space.

7. Using the 2½"-wide gold strips, make two strip sets of four strips each. Crosscut the strip sets into 16 segments, 2½" wide. Sew the crosscut segments into four units of three segments each. Sew one crosscut segment to each side of the panel sections from step 6. Press. Sew the pieced crosscut segments to the top and bottom. Press. Add the Rail Fence blocks. Press.

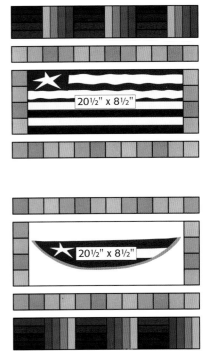

Make 1 of each.

8. With right sides together, place a red 1½" square on one corner of a light beige 1½" x 2½" rectangle. Draw a diagonal line through the center of the square as shown and stitch on the drawn line. Trim away the excess fabric, leaving a ¼" seam allowance. Press. Repeat on the other side of the rectangle. Press. Repeat, using the blue 1½" squares. Make eight red and eight blue flying-geese units.

9. Make two small Star blocks with red points and a blue center, and two with blue points and a red center as described in step 8 on page 30. Each block should measure 4½" x 4½".

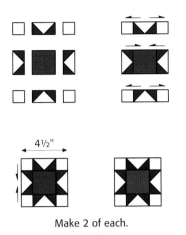

Make 2 of each.

10. Trim four smaller panel pieces (or a theme print) to 4½" x 4½".

CLEVER TIP

If you want to cut small panel pieces askew as I did, cut and add coping strips to make them slightly larger before cutting. You can also substitute Four Patch blocks made from 2½" squares for the 4½"-square areas.

11. Sew the units from step 10 to one side of the small Star blocks as shown.

Make 2 of each.

12. Using the gold 2½" squares and the light beige 2½" x 4½" rectangles, make eight flying-geese units for the large Star blocks as described in step 8.

13. Using the red and blue 2½" squares, make two Four Patch blocks for the center of the large Star blocks.

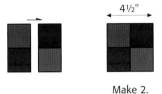

Make 2.

14. Sew two large Star blocks in the same manner as described in step 12 on page 31. The blocks should measure 8½" x 8½".

15. Trim two panel pieces to 4½" x 4½". Add the gold rectangles.

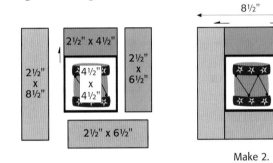

Make 2.

16. Trim four larger panel pieces to 8½" x 8½". Add blue filler strips if needed. Add the Rail Fence blocks. Press. Each unit should measure 12½" x 12½".

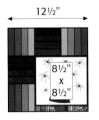

Make 1 of each.

17. Trim the remaining larger panel pieces to 6½" x 8½". Add coping or filler strips if needed. Add the reserved pieced segments from steps 3 and 4 as shown. Press. Each unit should measure 8½" x 12½".

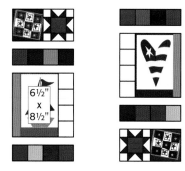

18. Sew the blocks from steps 11, 14, 15, and 17 together in two long vertical rows as shown in the quilt diagram. Press. Add the remaining Rail Fence blocks to the outer edges. Press.

19. Add the blocks from step 16 to the top and bottom of the units from step 18. Press.

20. Sew the quilt together in vertical rows as shown in the quilt diagram. Sew the rows together to form the quilt top.

21. Quilt as desired and bind. Refer to "Finishing Your Quilt" on page 18 for more details if needed. This quilt was machine quilted in gold thread using a combination of stars and a meandering stitch.

OTHER OPTIONS

Other types of panel prints, theme prints, or pieced blocks can easily be placed within the blank spaces allowed for the pictures and blocks in this quilt. Just be sure that the picture or block has the same measurement as the slot allowed. Add coping strips or triangles if needed. To accommodate a larger piece, you may also eliminate the Rail Fence blocks along the sides of the panel images.

Best Friends

Designed and sewn by Susan Dissmore, machine quilted by Sue Gantt, 2002.

About This Quilt

Finished quilt: 34" x 42"

Finished block: 4" x 4"

Designed to be a quick-and-easy baby shower gift, this quilt features a nostalgic theme print of children at play. The theme print is accented with a soft pastel palette of repeating prints in different colorways. This sweet quilt can be interpreted in countless different ways, depending on your choice of theme fabric.

Materials

Yardages are based on 42"-wide fabric.

♦ 1 yard of theme print for alternate blocks
♦ 1 fat quarter *each* of 4 lights in yellow, pink, blue, and green for Four Patch blocks
♦ 1 fat quarter *each* of 4 darks in yellow, pink, blue, and green for Four Patch blocks
♦ ¼ yard of blue print for inner border
♦ 1⅝ yards of fabric for backing
♦ ½ yard of fabric for binding
♦ 42" x 50" piece of batting

Cutting

All measurements include ¼" seam allowance.

From the theme print, selectively cut:

♦ 24 squares, 4½" x 4½"

From *each* of the light fabrics, cut:

♦ 4 strips, 2½" x 21"

From *each* of the dark yellow and dark blue fabrics, cut:

♦ 4 strips, 2½" x 21"

From *each* of the dark pink and dark green fabrics, cut:

♦ 5 strips, 2½" x 21"

From the blue print, cut:

♦ 2 strips, 1½" x 32½"
♦ 2 strips, 1½" x 26½"

Assembly

1. Pair each light yellow strip with a dark yellow strip. Repeat with the pink, blue, and green fabrics. Sew the strips together into 16 strip sets. Press to the dark fabric. Crosscut the strip sets into 2½"-wide segments. From each of the blue and yellow sets, cut 30 segments. From each of the green and pink sets, cut 26 segments.

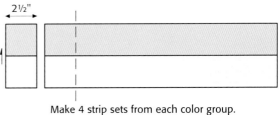

Make 4 strip sets from each color group.
Cut 30 yellow segments, 30 blue segments,
26 green segments, and 26 pink segments.

2. Using 12 segments from each color combination, sew six Four Patch blocks of each color. Press. The blocks should measure 4½" square.

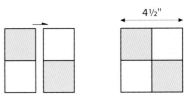

Make 6 of
each color.

3. Arrange and sew the theme print squares and the Four Patch blocks in rows as shown in the quilt diagram at right. Press toward the theme print squares. Sew the rows together.

4. Sew the 32½"-long blue print strips to each side of the quilt. Press.

5. Sew the 26½"-long blue print strips to the top and bottom of the quilt. Press.

6. Following the quilt diagram, sew the remaining 2½"-wide crosscut segments together into two sets of 13 for the top and bottom outer borders, and two sets of 17 for the side outer borders. Press and set aside.

7. Sew the remaining green and pink 2½" x 21" strips together to form a strip set. Crosscut the strip set into four 2½"-wide segments. Using the green-and-pink segments and the four remaining yellow segments, make 4 Four Patch blocks as shown. Press.

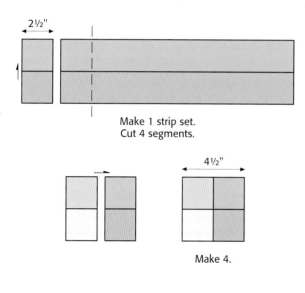

2½"

Make 1 strip set.
Cut 4 segments.

4½"

Make 4.

8. Sew the Four Patch blocks to each side of the top and bottom border rows as shown. Press toward the corner blocks.

9. Sew the side borders to the quilt. Then sew the top and bottom borders to the quilt. Press toward the inner border.

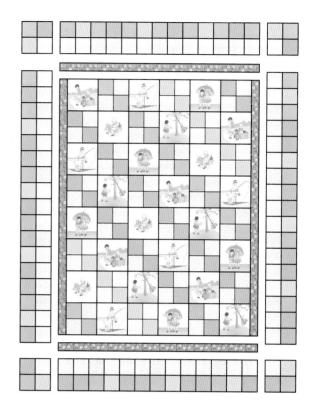

10. Quilt as desired and bind. Refer to "Finishing Your Quilt" on page 18 for more details if needed. This quilt was machine quilted using a crosshatch pattern in the center and a meandering stitch with butterflies in the border.

OTHER OPTIONS

- The theme print square can be easily replaced with any small panel square that has a finished size measurement up to 4" x 4".

- For an extra-special baby gift, accompany the quilt with a storybook or picture book that complements the theme fabric in the quilt.

Four Patch Magic

Designed by Susan Dissmore, sewn by Ginger Lundberg, machine quilted by Sue Gantt, 2002.

About This Quilt

Finished quilt: 50" x 66"
Finished block and large theme print square: 8" x 8"
Finished small theme print square: 4" x 4"

Since the Four Patch block is so easy, I took it one step further and made double Four Patch blocks! I combined a large-scale theme print featuring enchanted castles, princesses, and dragons with a smaller, coordinating theme print to create this cozy, quick-and-easy, lap-size flannel quilt.

Materials

Yardages are based on 42"-wide fabric.

- 1¾ yards of large-scale theme print
- 1 yard of small-scale theme print
- 2 yards of fabric for border
- ½ yard *each* of 2 coordinates for fabrics A and B in the Four Patch blocks
- 3½ yards of fabric for backing
- ⅝ yard of fabric for binding
- 58" x 74" piece of batting

Cutting

All measurements include ¼" seam allowance.

From the large-scale theme print, selectively cut:

- 18 squares, 8½" x 8½"

From the small-scale theme print, selectively cut:

- 34 squares, 4½" x 4½"

From *each* of fabrics A and B, cut:

- 5 strips, 2½" x 42"

From the border fabric, cut:

- 4 strips, 5½" x length of fabric

Assembly

1. Sew a fabric A strip to a fabric B strip to form a strip set. Press toward the darker fabric and repeat with the remaining fabric A and B strips. Cross-cut the strip sets into 68 segments, 2½" x 4½".

Make 5 strip sets.
Cut 68 segments.

2. Sew the crosscut segments together to make 34 Four Patch blocks that measure 4½" x 4½".

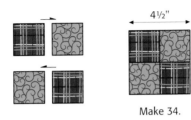

Make 34.

3. Using the Four Patch blocks from step 2 and the 4½" small-scale theme print squares, sew a larger Four Patch block. Press. Make 17 blocks that measure 8½" x 8½".

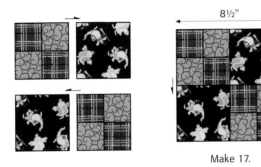

Make 17.

4. Using the blocks from step 3 and the 8½" large-scale theme print squares, sew the blocks together in rows, referring to the quilt diagram. Press the seams toward the theme print squares. Sew the rows together to form the quilt top.

5. Measure the quilt top from top to bottom and cut the side borders to that measurement. Sew the side borders to the quilt. Press toward the border.

6. Measure the quilt top from side to side and cut the top and bottom borders to that measurement. Sew the top and bottom borders to the quilt. Press.

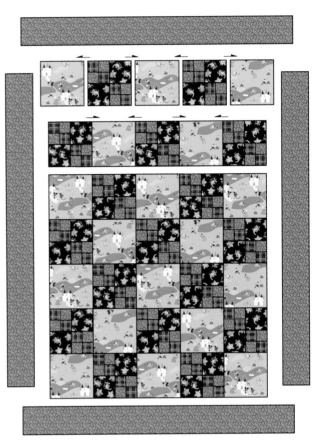

7. Quilt as desired and bind. Refer to "Finishing Your Quilt" on page 18 for more details if needed. This quilt was machine quilted with a castle design in the theme blocks and circular clouds in the Four Patch blocks.

OTHER OPTIONS

Replace the theme print with any panel print that has a finished-size measurement of up to 8" x 8". You could also add coping triangles around a theme print to achieve a new look for the quilt.

Birds of a Feather

Designed, sewn, and quilted by Susan Dissmore, 2002.

Materials

Yardages are based on 42"-wide fabric.

♦ 12 bird panels for block centers

♦ ½ yard of black print for borders

♦ ¼ yard *each* of 4 assorted blue prints for blocks and border

♦ ¼ yard *each* of 4 assorted red prints for blocks and border

♦ ¼ yard *each* of 4 assorted green prints for blocks and border

♦ ¼ yard *each* of 4 assorted gold prints for blocks and border

♦ 1⅝ yards of fabric for backing

♦ ½ yard of fabric for binding

♦ 40" x 51" piece of batting

Cutting

All measurements include ¼" seam allowance.

From the panel fabric, selectively cut:

♦ 12 rectangles, 5½" x 6"

From *each* of the blue, red, green, and gold prints, cut:

♦ 4 strips, 1½" x 42"

From the black print, cut:

♦ 8 strips, 1½" x 42"

♦ 4 rectangles, 1½" x 2½"*

You may want to cut these pieces later from scraps left over from the border strips.

Assembly

1. Sew a red strip to the top of three panel rectangles. Press the seam allowances away from the center, and trim the excess red fabric. Repeat to sew a red strip to the right side of each. Press and trim the excess red fabric.

2. Sew a blue strip to the bottom of the panel rectangles. Press the seam allowances away from the center, and trim the excess blue fabric. Repeat to sew a blue strip to the left side of each. Press and trim away the excess blue fabric.

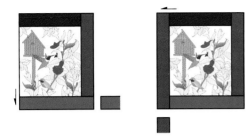

3. Repeat the above steps, adding one more round of "logs." When complete, you will have three blocks that should measure 9½" x 10". Trim if necessary. Repeat with the remaining colors in the combinations shown.

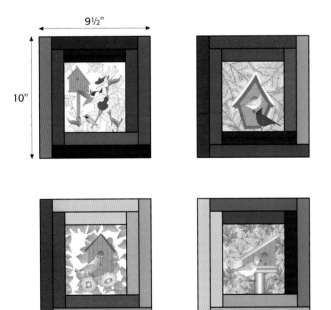

Make 3 of each color combination.

4. Referring to the quilt diagram, sew the blocks together in rows. Sew the rows together to form the quilt top.

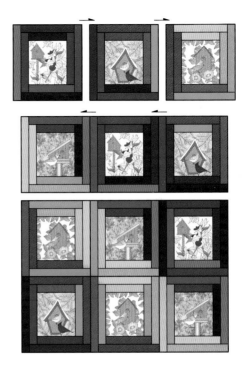

5. Measure the quilt top from top to bottom and cut two of the black border strips to that measurement. Sew the strips to the sides of the quilt top. Press.

6. Measure the quilt top from side to side and cut two of the black border strips to that measurement. Sew those strips to the top and bottom of the quilt top. Press.

7. Sew the remaining blue, red, green, and gold strips together into four strip sets of four strips each. Crosscut the strip sets into 39 segments, 2½" wide. Sew 10 segments together to form each side

border section. Sew 9 segments together for the top and bottom borders.

CLEVER TIP

Once you have sewn your crosscut segments together, measure them to ensure a nice fit. If the measurement is larger or smaller than desired, adjust your seam allowances until the desired measurement is achieved.

8. Measure the quilt top from top to bottom and cut two of the black border strips to that measurement. Sew these strips to the outside of the pieced side borders. Press toward the black strips. Sew the border units to the sides of the quilt top. Press.

9. Remove three of the 1½" x 2½" strips from one end of the top and bottom pieced border units so that there are 33 strips. Sew a 1½" x 2½" black rectangle to each end of the pieced border units. Press.

10. Measure the quilt top from side to side and cut the remaining black border strips to that measurement. Sew these strips to the pieced top and bottom borders as shown in the quilt diagram.

Press. Sew the border units to the top and bottom of the quilt. Press.

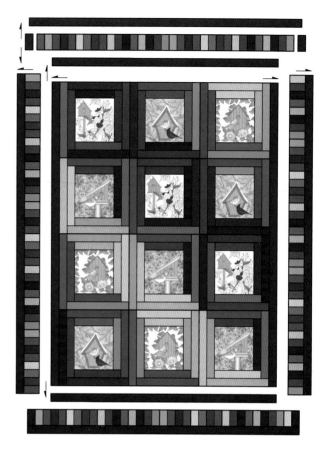

11. Quilt as desired and bind. Refer to "Finishing Your Quilt" on page 18 for more details if needed. This quilt was machine quilted using variegated thread and free-motion techniques to create flowers, leaves, and meandering stitches.

OTHER OPTIONS

Any theme print can be substituted for the panel picture used in this quilt. Also remember that a Log Cabin block is easily adjusted to fit any size square or rectangle just by changing the length of the strips added. The sewing technique remains the same; only the size changes.

Child's Play

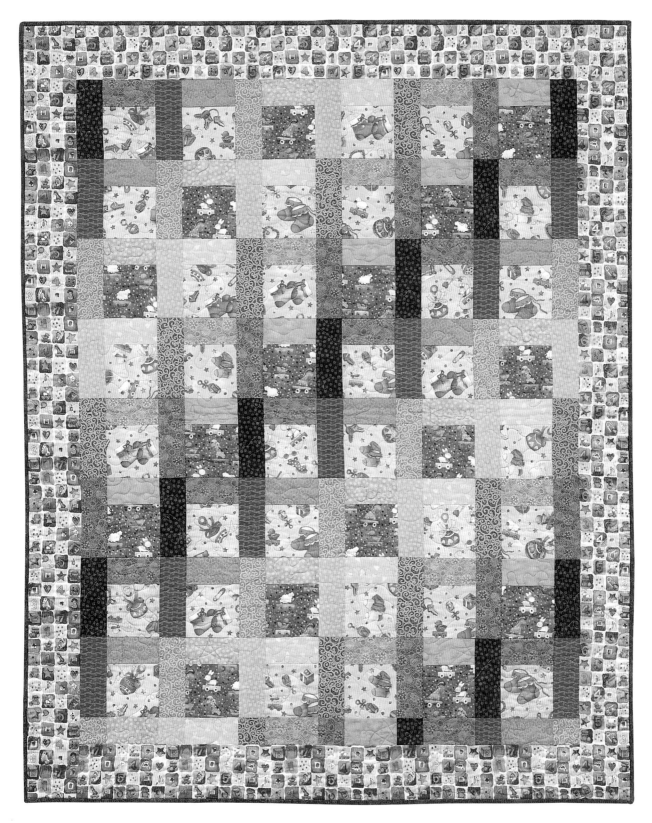

Designed by Susan Dissmore, sewn by Ginger Lundberg, machine quilted by Sue Gantt, 2002.

Materials

Yardages are based on 42"-wide fabric.

♦ ½ yard of pink theme print
♦ ½ yard of yellow theme print
♦ ½ yard of blue theme print
♦ 1⅞ yards of coordinating print for border
♦ 1 fat quarter *each* of 6 medium tone-on-tone fabrics in purple, blue, green, yellow, orange, and pink for lattice
♦ 1 fat quarter *each* of 6 dark tone-on-tone fabrics in purple, blue, green, yellow, orange, and pink for lattice
♦ 3 yards of fabric for backing
♦ ⅝ yard of fabric for binding
♦ 54" x 66" piece of batting

Cutting

All measurements include ¼" seam allowance.

From *each* of the 3 theme prints, selectively cut:

♦ 16 squares, 4½" x 4½"

From *each* of the 6 medium fat quarters, cut:

♦ 2 strips, 2½" x 21"
♦ 1 rectangle, 2½" x 4½"

From *each* of the 6 dark fat quarters, cut:

♦ 4 strips, 2½" x 21". Reserve 3 strips; from the fourth strip, cut:
  · 2 rectangles, 2½" x 6½", from purple and blue
  · 1 rectangle, 2½" x 6½", from each of the green, yellow, orange, and pink
  · 2 squares, 2½" x 2½", from green
  · 1 square, 2½" x 2½", from each of the purple, blue, yellow, orange, and pink

From the coordinating border print, cut:

♦ 5 strips, 4½" x length of fabric

Assembly

1. With right sides together, sew a pink theme print square to a medium purple 2½"-wide strip. Repeat until you have sewn eight of the squares to the strips.

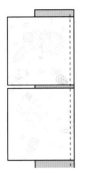

2. Press toward the strip and trim away the excess fabric using a rotary cutter and ruler.

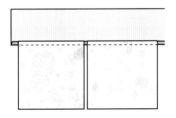

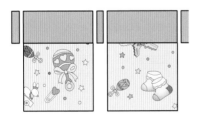

CLEVER TIP

After stitching the theme print squares to a 2½" strip, lay the unit on your ironing surface with the strip on top. Press the seam to set the stitches. Then flip the strip back and press again; the seam will be pressed toward the strip.

3. Sew the trimmed units from step 2 to a dark purple 2½"-wide strip. Press toward the strip and trim away the excess fabric. The blocks should measure 6½" square.

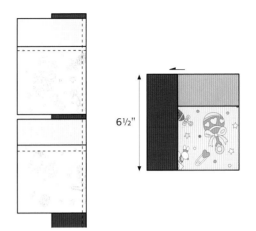

4. Repeat steps 1 and 2 to make eight of each of the blocks in the color combinations shown.

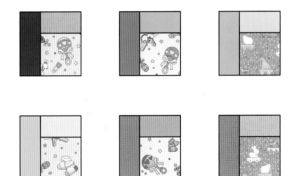

Make 8 of each color combination.

5. Sew the blocks together in rows, referring to the quilt diagram on page 52. Press the seams in opposite directions from row to row. Sew the rows together. Press the seams all in one direction.

6. Sew the dark 2½" x 6½" rectangles together, end to end, as shown in the quilt diagram for the right side of the quilt. Press seams in the opposite direction of the block rows so that the seams will butt. Sew to the right side of the quilt. Press toward the border.

7. Sew the dark 2½" squares to the medium 2½" x 4½" rectangles, end to end, as shown in the quilt diagram for the bottom row of the quilt. Press. Sew to the bottom of the quilt. Press.

8. Measure the quilt from side to side and cut two border strips to that measurement. Sew to the top and bottom of the quilt. Press.

9. Measure the quilt from top to bottom and cut two border strips to that measurement. Sew to the sides. Press.

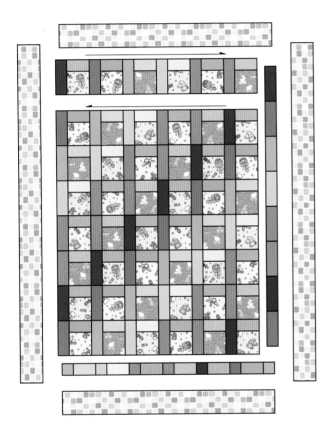

10. Quilt as desired and bind. Refer to "Finishing Your Quilt" on page 18 for more details if needed. This quilt was machine quilted in a meandering pattern that randomly includes stars and the words *mommy* and *baby*.

Frogs for the Boys

Designed and sewn by Susan Dissmore, machine quilted by Eileen Peacher, 2002.

About This Quilt

Finished quilt: 51" x 63" (Border Options One and Three)
Finished quilt: 47" x 59" (Border Option Two)
Finished block: 9" x 9"
Finished panel square: 5" x 5"

The first quilt in this series, "Boys Toys," was originally designed and made for my younger son a few years ago. It featured a car theme print. He just loved automobiles, and now at the age of 15, he loves the thought of driving them even more! If you need a quilt for that special guy in your life (who doesn't care how little time you spent), then this simple quilt is for you! It looks much more complex than it really is. There are three border options: a pieced border, a simple border, and a border that features a theme print. See the border options on page 56.

Materials

Yardages are based on 42"-wide fabric. See page 56 for border options.

♦ 1 yard of large-scale theme print for block centers
♦ **Option one:** ⅜ yard of small-scale theme print for pieced border
♦ **Option three:** 1 yard of small-scale theme print
♦ **All options:** 2 yards of fabric for unpieced border
♦ ⅝ yard of gold print for accents
♦ ½ yard of black print for block frames
♦ ⅜ yard *each* of 3 darks in red, green, and purple for blocks and sashings (½ yard *each* for option one)
♦ ⅜ yard *each* of 3 mediums in red, green, and purple for blocks and sashings (½ yard *each* for option one)
♦ 3½ yards of fabric for backing
♦ ⅝ yard of fabric for binding
♦ 59" x 71" piece of batting

Cutting

All measurements include ¼" seam allowance.

From the large-scale theme print, selectively cut:
♦ 12 squares, 5½" x 5½"

For *option one,* from the small-scale theme print, selectively cut:
♦ 18 squares, 3½" x 3½"

For *option three,* from the small-scale theme print, selectively cut:
♦ 8 strips, 2½" x 42"

From the black print, cut:
♦ 1 strip, 5½" x 42". From it, cut 24 rectangles, 1¼" x 5½"*.
♦ 1 strip, 6½" x 42". From it, cut 24 rectangles, 1¼" x 6½"*.

From the gold print, cut:
♦ 3 strips, 2" x 42". Cut the strips in half to yield 6 strips, 2" x 21".
♦ 2 strips, 3½" x 42". From them, cut 20 squares, 3½" x 3½".
♦ **Option one:** 4 squares, 3½" x 3½"

These rectangles are intentionally cut wider than necessary.

From *each* of the 3 medium fabrics, cut:

- 1 strip, 6½" x 42". Cut the strip in half to yield 2 strips, 6½" x 21"; reserve 1 strip; from the other strip, cut 8 rectangles, 2" x 6½".
- **Option one:** 2 strips, 1½" x 42"

From *each* of the 3 dark fabrics, cut:

- 1 strip, 9½" x 42". From the red, cut 11 rectangles, 3½" x 9½"; from each of the green and purple fabrics, cut 10 rectangles, 3½" x 9½".
- **Option one:** 2 strips, 1½" x 42"

From the border fabric, cut:

- **Option one:**   8 strips, 2" x length of fabric
  4 rectangles, 2" x 3½"
- **Option two:**   4 strips, 4½" x length of fabric
- **Option three:**   8 strips, 2½" x length of fabric

Quilt Top Assembly

1. Sew the 1¼" x 5½" black rectangles to the top and bottom of each large-scale theme print square. Press toward the frame fabric and trim to 5½" x 6½". Sew the 1¼" x 6½" black rectangles to the sides. Press and trim to 6½" x 6½".

6½"

Make 12.

2. Sew the 2" x 21" gold strips to each side of the reserved 6½" x 21" medium red, green, and purple strips. Press toward the 6½"-wide strips. Crosscut each unit into eight 2"-wide segments.

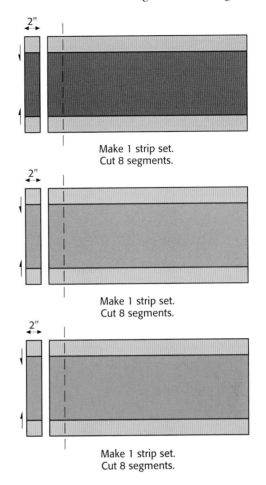

2"

Make 1 strip set.
Cut 8 segments.

2"

Make 1 strip set.
Cut 8 segments.

2"

Make 1 strip set.
Cut 8 segments.

3. Sew four of the medium green 2" x 6½" rectangles to the top of four of the units from step 1. Press. Sew four of the medium red 2" x 6½" rectangles to the bottom. Press. Sew four of the medium green-and-gold and medium red-and-gold crosscut segments from step 2 to the sides as shown. Press. The blocks should measure 9½" x 9½".

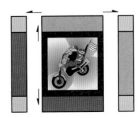 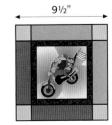

9½"

Make 4.

4. Repeat the above process using the remaining strips and crosscut segments to make the remaining eight blocks.

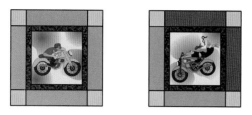

Make 4 of each color combination.

5. Using the blocks from steps 3 and 4 and a total of sixteen 3½" x 9½" rectangles (six dark red, five dark green, and five dark purple), sew the block rows together as shown in the quilt diagram. Press toward the dark strips.

6. Using the gold 3½" squares and the remaining dark red, green, and purple 3½" x 9½" rectangles, sew the sashing rows as shown in the quilt diagram. Press toward the dark strips.

7. Sew the block rows to the sashing rows. Press toward the sashing rows.

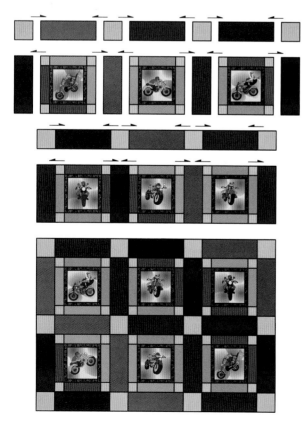

Border Assembly

Choose a border from one of the options shown below: a pieced border (option one), a plain border (option two), or a theme-print border (option three).

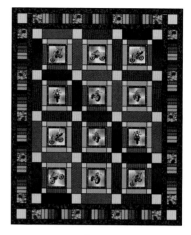

Option One

Option Two

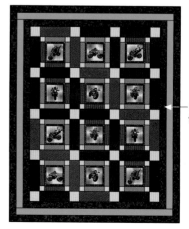

Small-scale theme print

Option Three

Option One

1. Using the 1½" x 42" medium and dark red, green, and purple strips, sew four strip sets with three strips in each set. Crosscut the strip sets into 42 segments, 3½" x 3½". Sew the segments together in 14 sets of three segments each (three sets each for the top and bottom and four sets each for the sides). Press the seams all in one direction.

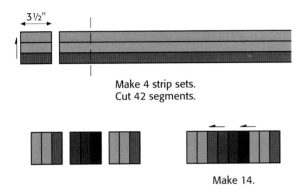

Make 4 strip sets.
Cut 42 segments.

Make 14.

2. Add the 3½" theme print squares to each side of the pieced units from step 1 as shown in the quilt diagram at right. Press in one direction.

3. Measure the quilt top from side to side, cut two of the 2"-wide border strips to that measurement, and sew to the top and bottom of the quilt. Press toward the border strip. Add the top and bottom pieced segments from step 2. Press.

4. Repeat step 3 for the sides, measuring the quilt from top to bottom.

5. Sew the 2" x 3½" border rectangles to the gold 3½" squares and add to the ends of the pieced segments from step 2. Press and add to the sides of the quilt top.

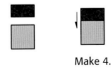

Make 4.

6. Repeat steps 3 and 4 using the remaining border strips. Press.

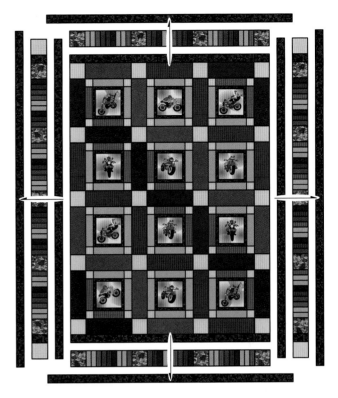

7. Quilt as desired and bind. Refer to "Finishing Your Quilt" on page 18 for more details if needed. This quilt was machine quilted in a lightning pattern using variegated thread.

Option Two

1. Measure the quilt from top to bottom, cut two of the 4½"-wide border strips to that measurement, and sew to the sides of the quilt. Press toward the border.

2. Measure the quilt from side to side, cut the remaining two 4½"-wide border strips to that measurement, and sew to the top and bottom of the quilt. Press toward the border.

3. Quilt as desired and bind. Refer to "Finishing Your Quilt" on page 18 for more details if needed.

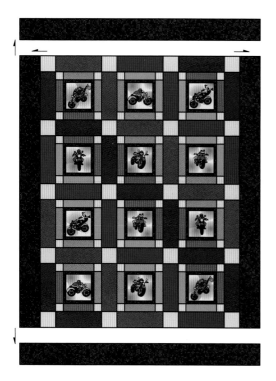

CLEVER TIP

If you want to add corner squares to the border, cut the squares to the same measurement as the width of your border strip.

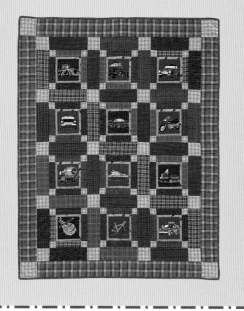

Option Three

1. Measure the quilt from top to bottom, cut two of the 2½"-wide border strips to that measurement, and sew to the sides of the quilt. Press toward the border.

2. Measure the quilt from side to side, cut two 2½"-wide border strips to that measurement, and sew to the top and bottom of the quilt. Press toward the border.

3. Piece the 2½"-wide small-scale theme print strips together, end to end, into four sets of two strips each. Repeat steps 1 and 2 using the pieced small-scale theme print strips. Press.

4. Repeat steps 1 and 2 using the remaining 2½"-wide border strips. Press.

5. Quilt as desired and bind. Refer to "Finishing Your Quilt" on page 18 for more details if needed.

Forever Friends

Designed, sewn, and quilted by Susan Dissmore, 2001.

About This Quilt

Finished quilt: 48" x 67"
Finished block: 14" x 14"
Finished panel square: $9\frac{7}{8}$" x $9\frac{7}{8}$"

This teddy bear fabric spoke to me the moment I saw it. The colors were so inviting and warm. Right away I went to the drawing board to create this captivating quilt. It is sure to warm your heart and home as well.

Materials

Yardages are based on 42"-wide fabric.

♦ 6 panels from panel print for block A
♦ ½ yard of theme print for block B and side triangles
♦ 2 yards of blue tone-on-tone print for border
♦ ⅞ yard of light beige print for triangles in block A
♦ ⅝ yard of blue print for larger triangles in B and setting-triangle units
♦ 5 assorted fat quarters of coordinating fabrics for strip-pieced units
♦ 1 fat quarter of plaid for smaller triangles in block B and setting-triangle units
♦ 3 yards of fabric for backing
♦ ⅝ yard of fabric for binding
♦ 56" x 75" piece of batting

Cutting

All measurements include ¼" seam allowance.

From the panel print, selectively cut:

♦ 6 panels, $10\frac{3}{8}$" x $10\frac{3}{8}$"

From the theme print, selectively cut:

♦ 2 squares, 4" x 4", on point*
♦ 4 rectangles, 3" x 5½" (vertical orientation)
♦ 2 rectangles, 5½" x 3" (horizontal orientation)

From the light beige print, cut:

♦ 3 strips, 8" x 42". From them, cut 12 squares, 8" x 8"; cut the squares in half diagonally once to yield 24 triangles.
♦ 4 squares, 3" x 3", from leftover pieces

From the blue print, cut:

♦ 2 strips, $8\frac{1}{4}$" x 42". From them, cut 6 squares, $8\frac{1}{4}$" x $8\frac{1}{4}$"; cut the squares in half diagonally twice to yield 24 triangles.
♦ 4 squares, $3\frac{3}{8}$" x $3\frac{3}{8}$", from leftover pieces. Cut the squares in half diagonally once to yield 8 triangles.

From *each* of the 5 assorted fat quarters, cut:

♦ 8 strips, 1½" x 21"

From the plaid fat quarter, cut:

♦ 2 strips, $4\frac{3}{4}$" x 21". From them, cut 5 squares, $4\frac{3}{4}$" x $4\frac{3}{4}$"; cut the squares in half diagonally twice to yield 20 triangles.
♦ 1 strip, $4\frac{3}{8}$" x 21". From this strip and the leftover $4\frac{3}{4}$"-wide strip from above, cut 7 squares, $4\frac{3}{8}$" x $4\frac{3}{8}$"; cut the squares in half diagonally once to yield 14 triangles.

From the blue tone-on-tone print, cut:

♦ 4 strips, 4½" x length of fabric

See page 15 for information about selective cutting on point.

Assembly

1. To make block A, sew the light beige triangles to each side of the panel square. Press toward the triangles. Trim the block to 14½" x 14½". Repeat to make six blocks.

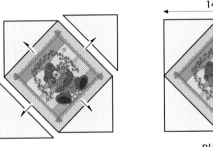

Block A
Make 6.

2. To make block B, begin by sewing the smaller blue print triangles to each side of the 4" theme print squares. Press and trim to 5½" square.

Make 2.

3. Sew the strips cut from the assorted fat quarters into eight strip sets of five strips each. Press the seams all in one direction. Crosscut the strip sets into 14 squares, 5½" x 5½", and 20 rectangles, 3" x 5½".

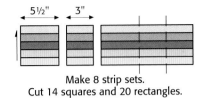

Make 8 strip sets.
Cut 14 squares and 20 rectangles.

4. Sew the larger blue print triangles to opposite sides of 10 of the 5½" pieced squares from step 3 as shown. Press toward the triangles. Sew a larger plaid triangle to the top to form a triangle unit. Press. Make 10 triangle units.

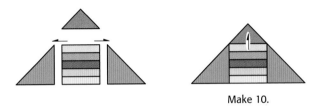

Make 10.

5. Sew the remaining 5½" pieced squares to each side of the blocks from step 2. Press. Sew a larger plaid triangle to each end. Press.

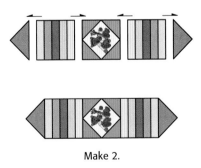

Make 2.

6. Sew two step 4 units to the unit from step 5 to form block B. Repeat to make two of block B. Press and trim to 14½" x 14½".

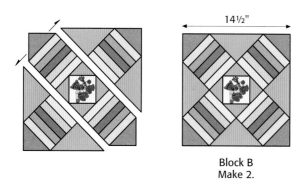

Block B
Make 2.

7. Sew the 3" x 5½" pieced rectangle units to each side of six 3" x 5½" theme print rectangles as shown. Press. Sew a smaller plaid triangle to each end. Press.

Make 6.

8. Sew the units from step 7 to the remaining units from step 4 to form the side triangle units. Press.

Make 6 side triangles.

9. Sew a larger blue print triangle to one side of a 3" x 5½" pieced rectangle unit. Sew a smaller plaid triangle to the end to make a triangle unit. Press. Make four units.

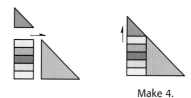

Make 4.

10. Sew a light beige 3" square and a smaller plaid triangle to opposite ends of the remaining four 3" x 5½" pieced rectangle units. Press.

Make 4.

11. Sew the units from steps 9 and 10 together to form the corner triangle units.

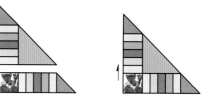

Make 4 corner triangles.

12. Referring to the quilt diagram on page 63, lay out the blocks, side triangles, and corner triangles to form the quilt top. Sew the blocks together in diagonal rows. Press. Sew the rows together.

13. Measure the quilt top from top to bottom and cut two side borders to that measurement. Sew the side borders to the quilt top. Press toward the borders.

14. Measure the quilt top from side to side and cut the remaining border strips to that measurement. Sew the top and bottom borders to the quilt. Press.

15. Quilt as desired and bind. Refer to "Finishing Your Quilt" on page 18 for more details if needed. This quilt was machine quilted using purple thread in random designs of flowers, leaves, vines, and petals.

Garden Hearts

Designed and sewn by Susan Dissmore, machine quilted by Eileen Peacher, 2002.

Materials

Yardages are based on 42"-wide fabric.

- 6 panels from panel print
- 2⅝ yards of green plaid for Heart blocks and outer border
- ¾ yard of blue print for Heart blocks
- ¾ yard of pink print for Heart blocks, panel blocks, and inner border
- ½ yard of light print for background of Heart blocks
- ½ yard of yellow tone-on-tone print for Heart and panel blocks
- ¼ yard *each* of blue tone-on-tone and green tone-on-tone prints for panel blocks
- 3½ yards of fabric for backing
- ⅝ yard of fabric for binding
- 60" x 74" piece of batting

Cutting

All measurements include ¼" seam allowance.

From the panel print, selectively cut:

- 6 rectangles, 14½" x 10½"

From the yellow tone-on-tone print, cut:

- 5 strips, 2½" x 42"

From the pink print, cut:

- 1 strip, 5" x 42". From it, cut 6 rectangles, 5" x 6½".
- 1 strip, 3" x 42". From it, cut 6 squares, 3" x 3"; cut the squares in half diagonally once to yield 12 triangles.
- 2 strips, 2½" x 42"
- 6 strips, 1½" x 42"

From *each* of the blue and green tone-on-tone prints, cut:

- 2 strips, 2½" x 42"

From the light print, cut:

- 2 squares, 4¼" x 4¼". Cut the squares in half diagonally twice to yield 8 triangles (2 are extra).
- 1 strip, 3½" x 42". From it, cut 12 squares, 3½" x 3½".
- 1 strip, 2⅜" x 42". From it, cut 6 squares, 2⅜" x 2⅜"; cut the squares in half diagonally once to yield 12 triangles.

From the green plaid, cut:

- 2 strips, 6½" x 42". Reserve 1 strip; from the remaining strip, cut 12 rectangles, 2½" x 6½".
- 4 strips, 4½" x length of remaining fabric (after cutting above pieces)

From the blue print, cut:

- 2 strips, 10½" x 42". Reserve 1 strip; from the remaining strip, cut 12 rectangles, 2½" x 10½".

Give Me Liberty

Designed and sewn by Susan Dissmore, machine quilted by Eileen Peacher, 2002.

About This Quilt

Finished quilt: 50" x 70"
Finished block: 10" x 10"
Finished panel square: 10" x 10"

Celebrate our freedom with red-white-and-blue fabrics pieced into Half Log Cabin and Star blocks. Add the patriotic bear panel print just for fun! Or choose almost any other theme fabric to fill the spaces. It may look complex, but the blocks are surprisingly simple and easy to make.

Materials

Yardages are based on 42"-wide fabric.

- 6 panels from panel fabric
- 1 yard of border print for outer blocks
- 1 yard of theme print for Star block centers
- 1 yard of light print for Star block background
- ⅞ yard of red print for Star block points
- ½ yard *each* of 4 assorted blue prints for Half Log Cabin blocks
- ½ yard of plaid for Star block centers
- 1 fat quarter *each* of 4 assorted light prints for Half Log Cabin blocks
- 3¼ yards of fabric for backing
- ⅝ yard of fabric for binding
- 58" x 78" piece of batting

Cutting

All measurements include ¼" seam allowance.

From the panel fabric, selectively cut:

- 6 squares, 10½" x 10½"

From the border print, selectively cut:

- 4 rectangles, 10½" x 5½" (horizontal orientation)
- 6 rectangles, 5½" x 10½" (vertical orientation)

From the theme print, selectively cut:

- 12 squares, 5½" x 5½"

From *each* of the 4 assorted blue prints, cut:

- 5 strips, 1¾" x 42"
- 1 strip, 3⅜" x 42". From it, cut 6 squares, 3⅜" x 3⅜"; cut the squares in half diagonally once to yield 12 triangles (total of 48).

From *each* of the 4 assorted light fat quarters, cut:

- 7 strips, 1¾" x 21"

From the light print, cut:

- 2 strips, 3⅜" x 42". From them, cut 24 squares, 3⅜" x 3⅜"; cut the squares in half diagonally once to yield 48 triangles.
- 7 strips, 3" x 42". From them, cut 48 rectangles, 3" x 5½".

From the plaid, cut:

- 4 strips, 3" x 42". From them, cut 48 squares, 3" x 3".

From the red print, cut:

- 8 strips, 3" x 42". From them, cut 96 squares, 3" x 3".

Assembly

Note that the diagrams below show fabric with the right sides facing up. When pressing the units for the Half Log Cabin blocks, press seams toward the strip just added.

1. Cut three of the 1¾" x 42" blue strips in half. Sew a 1¾" x 21" light strip and a 1¾" x 21" blue strip together to form a strip set. Press toward the blue fabric. Make five strip sets. Crosscut them into 48 segments, 1¾" x 3".

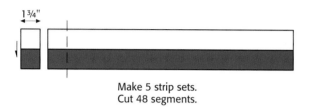

Make 5 strip sets.
Cut 48 segments.

2. With right sides together, sew the units from step 1 to the 1¾"-wide blue strips. Press, cut apart, and trim each unit to 3" square.

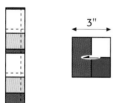

CLEVER TIP

Be sure to trim and square up the unit after each log is added. It's easy for the block to "grow" or become lopsided if you don't.

---

3. With right sides together, sew the units from step 2 to the light strips. Press, cut apart, and trim each unit to 3" x 4¼".

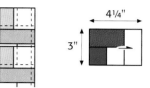

4. Continue adding blue and then light strips in the same manner. Trim to the sizes indicated in the diagrams below. Make 48 Half Log Cabin blocks.

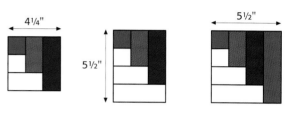

Make 48.

5. Sew four Half Log Cabin blocks together as shown to form a larger block. Make seven larger blocks.

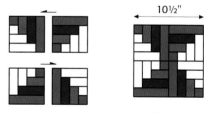

Make 7.

6. Using the border print rectangles and the remaining Half Log Cabin blocks, make the outer blocks; carefully place the border pieces in the direction shown.

Make 2.

Make 2.

Make 3.

Make 3.

7. Sew the light and blue print triangles together along the long edges. Press and trim to 3" square if needed.

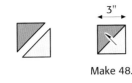

3"

Make 48.

8. With right sides together, place a 3" plaid square on one corner of the 5½" theme print square. Draw a diagonal line through the plaid square and then sew on the line. Trim away the excess fabric, leaving a ¼" seam allowance. Press toward the triangle. Repeat this process on each corner of the theme print square.

5½"

Make 12.

9. With right sides together, place a 3" red square on one corner of a light print 3" x 5½" rectangle. Draw a diagonal line through the red square and then sew on the line. Trim away the excess fabric, leaving a ¼" seam allowance. Press toward the light print. Repeat on the other corner of the rectangle. Press. Make 48 units.

5½"

3"

10. Sew the units from steps 7, 8, and 9 together in rows. Sew the rows together to make the Star block. Press. Make 12 blocks that measure 10½" x 10½".

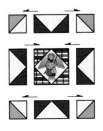 

10½"

Make 12.

11. Referring to the quilt diagram below, arrange the blocks into rows. Sew the blocks together. Press. Sew the rows together. Press.

12. Quilt as desired and bind. Refer to "Finishing Your Quilt" on page 18 for more details if needed. This quilt was machine quilted with a combination of meandering stitches and a zigzag pattern.

OTHER OPTIONS

Replace the panel print with any theme print that has a finished measurement of 10" x 10"; or simply make six more Star blocks. Experiment with other types of fabric for the outer blocks to create a whole new look for your quilt.

Once upon a Time

Designed and sewn by Susan Dissmore, machine quilted by Sue Gantt, 2002.

About This Quilt

Finished quilt: 58" x 70"
Finished block: 12" x 12"
Finished panel: 7" x 10"

Once upon a time there was a princess locked up high in a castle. She waited and waited in despair until one day her Prince Charming came riding up on a dragon to save her. Delighted with the prince by her side, she danced, sang, and smiled all the remaining days of her life. This quilt features those lovely rectangular panels that were intended to be a cloth book. Although a book is nice when telling a story, a quilt is a warm addition. It's like having a steamy cup of hot chocolate on a cold winter day! So, when you see these types of panels, think about buying two sets—one for a book and one for a quilt!

Materials

Yardages are based on 42"-wide fabric.

◆ 10 panels from panel fabric for block A
◆ ½ yard of theme print for block B
◆ 2 yards of blue print for outer border
◆ ⅞ yard of light print for block B background
◆ ½ yard of black print for block A coping strips
◆ ⅜ yard of green print for inner border
◆ 10 fat quarters of assorted brights for block B
◆ 3¾ yards of fabric for backing
◆ ⅝ yard of fabric for binding
◆ 66" x 78" piece of batting

Cutting

All measurements include ¼" seam allowance.

From the panel fabric, selectively cut:

◆ 10 rectangles, 7½" x 10½"

From the theme print, selectively cut:

◆ 10 squares, 4½" x 4½"

From the black print, cut:

◆ 5 strips, 1½" x 42". From them, cut 20 pieces, 1½" x 8½".
◆ 7 strips, 1" x 42". From them, cut 20 pieces, 1" x 10½".

From *each* of the assorted bright fat quarters, cut:

◆ 2 strips, 5¼" x 21". From them, cut a total of 45 squares, 5¼" x 5¼"; cut the squares in half diagonally twice to yield 180 triangles.
◆ 2 strips, 2⅞" x 21". From them, cut a total of 140 squares, 2⅞" x 2⅞"; cut the squares in half diagonally once to yield 280 triangles.

From the light print, cut:

◆ 4 strips, 3⅜" x 42". From them, cut 40 squares, 3⅜" x 3⅜".
◆ 2 strips, 5¼" x 42". From them, cut 10 squares, 5¼" x 5¼"; cut the squares in half diagonally twice to yield 40 triangles.

From the green print, cut:

◆ 6 strips, 1½" x 42"

From the blue print, cut:

◆ 4 strips, 4½" x length of fabric

Assembly

1. Sew the 1" x 10½" black coping strips to each side of the panel print. Press. Sew the 1½" x 8½" coping strips to the top and bottom. Press. The blocks should measure 8½" x 12½".

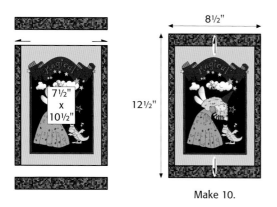

Make 10.

2. With right sides together, sew the short edges of two larger bright triangles together, offsetting the triangles and using a ¼" seam as shown. Press. Repeat to make 40 units of varying color combinations.

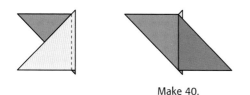

Make 40.

3. Sew the units into 20 sets of two units each in the same manner as described in step 2. Sew an additional triangle to one end. Press. Sew the smaller triangles to each end. Vary the color combinations as you sew. Press and trim the "dog ears," the little triangles of fabric that extend beyond the seam allowances.

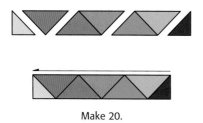

Make 20.

4. Sew the units from step 3 to each side of the units from step 1 to make block A. Press toward the coping strips. The blocks should measure 12½" x 12½".

Block A
Make 10.

5. With right sides together, sew two of the small bright triangles together along the shorter edges as shown. Make 40 units of varying color combinations. Press.

Make 40.

6. Sew a small bright triangle to one side of a light triangle. Press toward the small triangle and repeat on the other side. Repeat to make 40 units of varying color combinations.

Make 40.

7. Sew a small bright triangle to each side of 20 of the units from step 6, varying the colors. Press toward the small triangles. Sew 20 of the units from step 5 to the top. Press.

Make 20.

8. Sew the remaining 20 units from steps 5 and 6 together. Press. Sew these units to opposite sides of the 10 theme print squares. Press toward the squares.

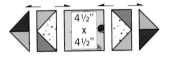

Make 10.

9. Sew the units from steps 7 and 8 together.

Make 10.

10. Sew the large bright triangles to each side of the 40 light squares. Press toward the triangles. Sew a smaller triangle to the top. Press.

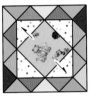

Make 40.

11. Sew the units from step 10 to the sides of the blocks from step 9 to make block B. Press. The blocks should measure 12½" x 12½".

12½"

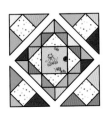

Block B
Make 10.

12. Sew blocks A and B together in rows as shown in the quilt diagram. Press the seams in opposite directions from row to row.

13. Sew the rows together. Press the seams all in one direction.

14. Sew two sets of three inner border strips together, end to end, to form two long strips. Measure the quilt from top to bottom and cut the side borders from one of the long strips to that measurement. Sew the side borders to the quilt. Press.

15. Measure the quilt from side to side and, from the remaining long strip, cut the inner top and bottom borders to that measurement. Sew to the top and bottom of the quilt. Press.

16. Measure the quilt from top to bottom and cut two of the outer border strips to that measurement. Sew to the sides of the quilt. Press. Measure the quilt top from side to side and cut the remaining two outer border strips to that measurement. Sew to the top and bottom of the quilt. Press.

17. Quilt as desired and bind. Refer to "Finishing Your Quilt" on page 18 for more details if needed. This quilt was machine quilted using gold thread in a meandering pattern.

Just Ducky

*48" x 58", designed by Susan Dissmore,
sewn and quilted by Lorri Gellerson, 2002.*

A slight modification to the panel print blocks (block A) changes the rectangular space into a square for the panel or theme print. In this quilt, I chose a brightly colored duck print as the feature fabric and made fewer blocks. You will need only six panel or theme print squares for this smaller version of "Once upon a Time." Cut them 8½" x 8½". Make six each of blocks A and B.

Block A Assembly

1. Follow step 2 on page 74 to make 24 triangle units in varying color combinations.

2. Sew one large triangle to one end. Press. Sew a small triangle to each end, varying the color combinations. Press and trim the dog ears.

3. Varying the colors, sew a small bright triangle and a light print triangle together to make 24 half-square-triangle units. Press.

Make 24.

4. Sew the half-square-triangle units to each side of 12 of the units from step 2. Press.

Make 12.

5. Sew the remaining units from step 2 to each side of the panel squares. Press toward the panel. Sew the units from step 4 to the top and bottom. Press. The blocks should measure 12½" x 12½".

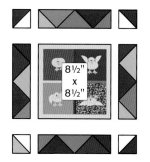

Make 6.

Versailles

Designed by Susan Dissmore, sewn and machine quilted by Sue Gantt, 2001.

About This Quilt

Finished quilt: 54½" x 68"
Finished block: 6" x 6"
Finished border-stripe width: 7¼"

It's always fascinating to see what can be done with the humble Nine Patch block. Here I've paired it with a wonderful French border print to create a simply elegant quilt in a vertical, strippy setting. Have fun experimenting with this one. You'll be amazed at how many different looks you can get with various border prints and coordinating fabrics for the Nine Patch blocks. Enjoy!

Materials

Yardages are based on 42"-wide fabric.

- 2¼ yards of floral border stripe
- 12 assorted fat quarters for Nine Patch blocks
- 1¼ yards of light print for setting triangles
- 3½ yards of fabric for backing
- ⅝ yard of fabric for binding
- 63" x 76" piece of batting

Cutting

All measurements include ¼" seam allowance.

From the border stripe, cut:

- 4 strips, approximately 7¾" x length of fabric

From *each* of the 12 fat quarters, cut:

- 6 strips, 2½" x 21"

From the light print, cut:

- 11 squares, 9¾" x 9¾". Cut the squares in half diagonally twice to yield 44 triangles (2 are extra).
- 6 squares, 5⅛" x 5⅛". Cut the squares in half diagonally once to yield 12 triangles.

Assembly

1. Sew the 2½"-wide strips into 24 strip sets of three strips each. Press 16 strip sets with the seam allowances toward the outer strips and 8 strip sets with the seams toward the middle strip. Crosscut the strip sets into 72 segments, 2½" wide. Note that you will have more strip sets than actually needed. This will give you more variety when combining segments.

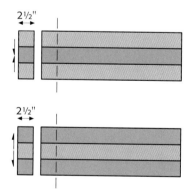

2. Make 24 Nine Patch blocks using the segments from step 1.

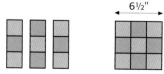

Make 24.

3. Sew the larger light triangles to each side of 18 Nine Patch blocks as shown. Press toward the triangles.

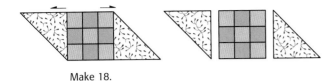

Make 18.

4. Sew a larger light triangle to one side of the remaining Nine Patch blocks as shown. Press.

Make 6.

5. Sew the units from steps 3 and 4 together to form the vertical rows as shown in the quilt diagram.

6. Sew the smaller light triangles to the ends of each row. Press.

7. Sew the border stripe fabric to the left side of each of the block rows. Press.

8. Add the final border stripe to the right side of one of the block rows. Sew the rows together.

9. Quilt as desired and bind. Refer to "Finishing Your Quilt" on page 18 for more details if needed. This quilt was quilted with a vertical design in the border panels and a meandering stitch around the Nine Patch blocks.

OTHER OPTIONS

Replace the Nine Patch block with a theme print or panel square. Because the blocks are set on point, consider adding coping triangles to the sides of the squares, in addition to side setting triangles. Then the blocks would be set straight. The width of the border stripe can vary from the 7¼" finished size. It can range from approximately 6½" to 8" wide. You could also use different stripes from the same fabric if they're available.

ABOUT THE AUTHOR

SUSAN TEEGARDEN DISSMORE began quilting in 1994 after opening a fabric shop specializing in dressmaking fabrics and garment sewing. The shop evolved as customers asked for quilting fabrics and supplies. Susan began to design her own quilts for exclusive use at the shop. She loves the design process and delights in using scraps in most of her quilt projects.

Susan was born and raised in eastern Washington. She owns and operates Sues Rags Quilt Shop in her current hometown of Federal Way, Washington, and is also a nonpracticing certified public accountant. She and her husband, Tim, have two sons, Blake and Justin, and a dog named Goldie.

YOU CAN FIND SUSAN AT:

Sues Rags Quilt Shop
1520 South Dash Point Road
Federal Way, WA 98003
(253) 941-5076
(888) 844-7247
www.suesrags.com